THE
HAROLD E. COOK
COLLECTION
OF
MUSICAL INSTRUMENTS

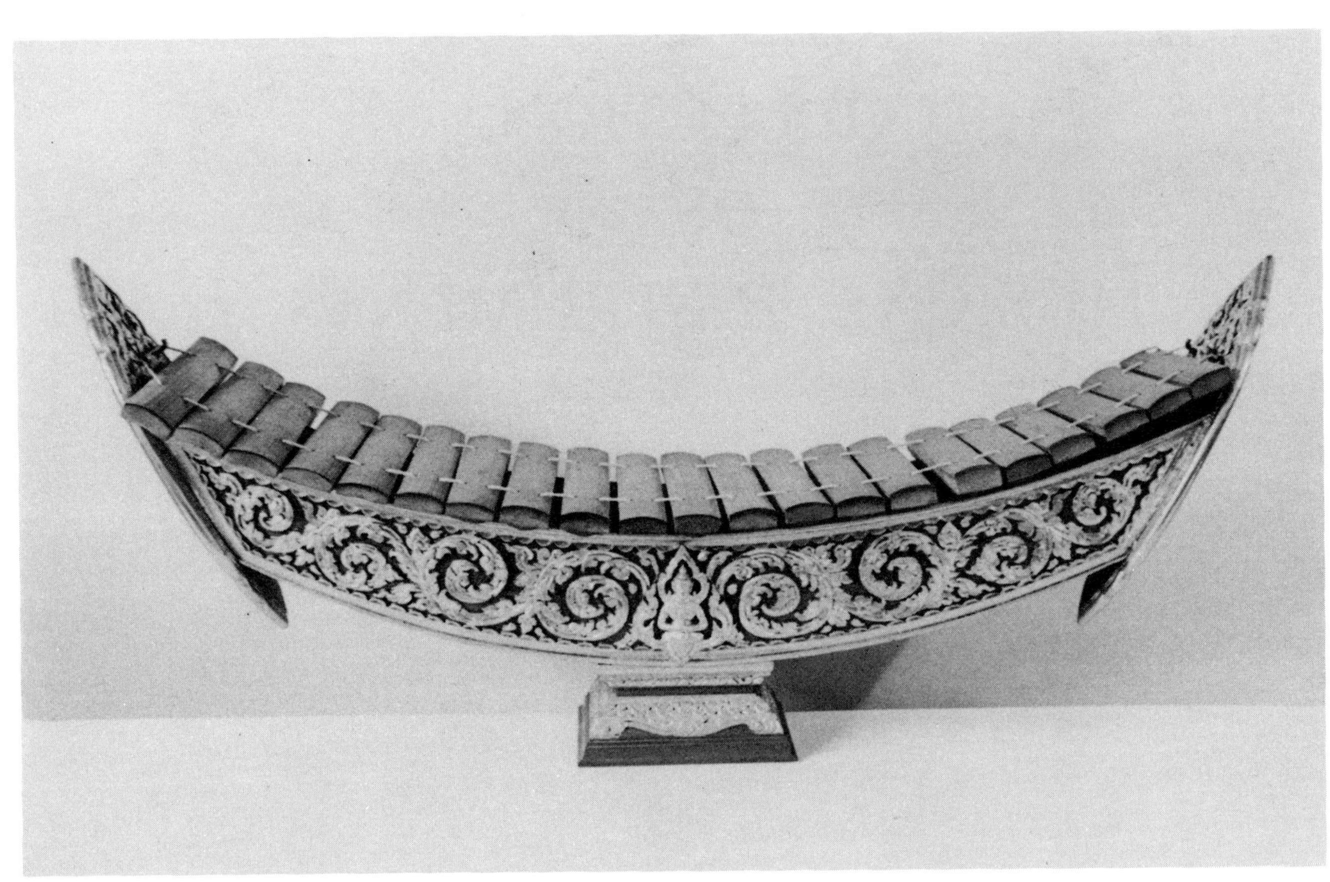

Frontispiece: no. 141. Xylophone, Thailand

THE HAROLD E. COOK COLLECTION OF MUSICAL INSTRUMENTS

Jackson Hill

LEWISBURG
BUCKNELL UNIVERSITY PRESS
LONDON: ASSOCIATED UNIVERSITY PRESSES

Associated University Presses, Inc.
Cranbury, New Jersey 08512

Associated University Presses
108 New Bond Street
London W1Y OQX, England

Library of Congress Cataloging in Publication Data
Hill, Jackson, 1941–
The Harold E. Cook collection of musical instruments.

Bibliography: p.
Includes indexes.
1. Musical instruments—Catalogs and collections.
I. Title.
ML462.L54B8   781.9'1'074014848   74–4837
ISBN 0–8387–1574–5

Contents

List of Illustrations

Preface

The purpose of this catalogue is to provide visitors to the collection with a useful reference source describing the instruments, and to serve to introduce the collection to a wider circle of musicians, organologists, and historians who have a general interest in musical instruments. This dual role is served by the inclusion of a discussion of the classification of instruments for the general reader, as well as detailed descriptions of the instruments for the more advanced investigator.

The primary function of the collection is its display and use in connection with Bucknell University's course offerings in the history of music, Asian music, and world folk music. At the present time, more than seventy percent of the collection is in playing condition, and more instruments will be repaired and restored as funds permit. This catalogue does not attempt to list all musical instruments at Bucknell, whose department of music also maintains a separate group of instruments essential to an active *collegium musicum.* Rather, this listing includes only those instruments that are part of the collection of the late Professor Harold E. Cook, presented to the university in 1970 by his wife, Gladys Calkins Cook, Professor of French.

A word is in order here concerning cataloguing procedure. The catalogue number of each instrument is given as the first item of each entry, along the left-hand margin, followed by the names by which the instrument is known. In most cases the most widely recognized name appears first, followed by equivalent names in parentheses. Names of variant instruments, instruments of which the listed item is itself a variant, and similar instruments appear in square brackets. Spellings, of course, are a matter of much variation and disagreement. Instrument names in this catalogue, however, use spellings that appear to the author to be the ones most commonly accepted.

The provenance, or locale in which the instrument is normally found, is followed in the listing by a general description that includes occasional historical information about the particular instrument, along with the location and date of collection or purchase.

Dimensions are given in both centimeters and inches, the largest dimension usually given first. Some confusion may necessarily result from some designations, as, for example, in describing the longest dimension of a horizontally held cylindrical drum as depth rather than as length. However, the following system and abbreviation scheme apply to this catalogue:

L: overall length (the longest dimension, usually horizontal)
W: width (the greatest horizontal dimension perpendicular to length, or the widest horizontal frontal dimension in upright instruments)
D: depth (a vertical dimension in box-shaped instruments; the distance from head-to-base or head-to-head in drums)
d: diameter
B: length of bow (in stringed instruments)

Following the letter abbreviation is given the measurement in centimeters; the equivalent in inches follows in parentheses.

In describing the pitch and range of particular instruments, the following scheme is employed. Octave designations run from C upward to B.

Assistance in preparing this catalogue has come from many quarters. The compiler is especially indebted to Jean Jenkins, The Horniman Museum, London, and to Richard Rephann, The Yale Collection of Musical Instruments, New Haven, for numerous helpful comments and welcome instruction.

History of the Collection

The year of Harold and Gladys Cook's first around-the-world trip, 1961, may be said to mark the beginning of the Cook Collection. Yet even before then, Professor Cook had long been interested in exotic music and had planned to offer a course in Oriental music at Bucknell. He was responsible for the university's acquisition of books and recordings related to ethnomusicology and was responsible for laying the groundwork for the current course offerings at Bucknell in Asian music and world folk music. His important study, *Shaker Music*, published by the Bucknell University Press, is further evidence of his scholarly inquiry into ethnomusicological topics.

Harold E. Cook was born in St. Mary's, West Virginia, July 7, 1904. He displayed considerable musical talent at an early age and left St. Mary's to study at Oberlin Conservatory, from which he received the Bachelor of Music degree in 1927. He spent the next year in Paris studying with Philippe and Robert Casadesus.

On his return to the United States, he accepted a teaching post at Franklin College in Indiana, remaining there for three years before returning to Oberlin to complete the Master of Music degree in piano.

In 1933, Harold Cook joined the staff of Bucknell University, where he remained until his death on December 18, 1967. He received the Ph.D. degree in musicology from Western Reserve University in 1947. At Bucknell, he was a full professor from 1950 until his death, and he was chairman of the Department of Music from 1948 to 1954.

In 1942, Harold Cook married Gladys E. Calkins, a professor in the French Department at Bucknell. Both of the Cooks were interested in art objects, indulging their passion for collecting things wherever they went, and they traveled widely.

As early as 1950, the Cooks were building an enviable collection of rare books and manuscripts, and when their around-the-world trips began in 1961, two other collections were initiated—musical instruments and oriental art.

As a result of their 1961 trip, which took the Cooks to Japan, Hong Kong, Malaysia, Thailand, India, Kashmir, Nepal, Afghanistan, Iraq, Iran, Lebanon, and Egypt, a room was needed in which to keep the growing number of musical instruments. A bedroom in their Lewisburg home was commandeered for use as an instrument gallery in much the same way that other areas of the house had been adapted to display Oriental statuary and to accommodate shelves of early editions in leather bindings.

In 1963 the Cooks undertook an extended tour of Africa, at which time they brought back home more instruments for the collection. Their second around-the-world trip, in 1965, included visits to Iran, Afghanistan, Pakistan, Nepal, India, Thailand, Hong Kong, and Japan; and the following year they visited the Philippines, Japan, Korea, South India, Iran, and Turkey.

Before and between these trips, however, the Cooks frequently traveled in Europe, and it was during these shorter trips that many of the French, German, Italian, and Greek instruments were obtained.

Most of the instruments in the collection were purchased in small shops and bazaars. A few, notably the Pungi (561) and the raft zither (601), were collected in the field, and similarly, a few were obtained from galleries and commercial dealers.

By 1967, the collection had grown to more than one hundred fifty instruments, and it included representative instruments from all parts of the Eastern hemisphere, with the exceptions of Indonesia and Oceania. In 1970 the collection was presented to the Department of Music at Bucknell, for use in connection with its course offerings in music history and ethnic music. The collection is currently maintained by Bucknell University and may be seen by appointment upon application to the curator.

THE
HAROLD E. COOK
COLLECTION
OF
MUSICAL INSTRUMENTS

The Classification
of Musical Instruments

This section will serve to introduce the principal types and categories of instruments to the general reader by referring to specific instruments in the Cook Collection. Numerous classifications have been published that go into greater detail than is possible here, and the more advanced student is directed to such sources as those listed in the bibliography.

It should be apparent to the student of musical instruments that in all periods of history and in all regions of the world, man has employed materials close at hand in making his musical instruments. In many instances, these materials provide a workable basis for classifying various types of instruments, but in other instances systems of classification based on materials of construction produce only confusion.

The traditional division of the modern symphony orchestra into strings, woodwinds, brasses, and percussion—a system based largely upon materials of construction—is insufficient for any truly systematic cataloguing of instruments, even though on the surface we may know perfectly well what each one of these categories means. For example, the flute, although now made of metal, is considered to be a woodwind, and the piano, which sounds by means of strings, is considered a percussion instrument.

More successful perhaps is the traditional Chinese system, which divides instruments into eight groups: metal (101),[1] stone, silk (611, 623, 643), bamboo (513, 515), calabash (402, 403), terra cotta, skin (345, 346, 351), and wood (171). But even here, construction practices have evolved over the years and have rendered this system completely accurate only in a broad historical sense.

1. Three-digit numbers throughout refer to the numbers of individual instruments in the catalogue listing.

With an increase in interest in ethnic music in this century has come the need to more fully understand both the role of music in society and the use of musical instruments in many diversified cultural settings. With such broad, cross-cultural factors involved, the system of instrument classification devised early in this century by Erich von Hornbostel and Curt Sachs has become almost universally regarded as the most efficient for dealing with all types of musical instruments.[2] The Sachs-Hornbostel system categorizes instruments according to acoustical properties by defining the vibrating medium in each instance and by describing the action that causes the instrument to sound.

IDIOPHONES

The first division in the Sachs-Hornbostel system comprises the idiophones, instruments in which the vibrating medium is the instrument body itself without resort to additional structural features, such as skins, strings, or reeds. Many idiophones serve a primarily rhythmic function, as is the case with regard to many slit drums (171, 174) and cymbals (126, 129), although just as many serve a melodic role, as in the case of the xylophones (141, 145) and sansas (246, 247). Other idiophones that are struck (percussion) or struck together (concussion) include bells, clappers, jingles, and certain types of drums.

Bells can be made of metal (101, 103), wood (111), or other materials, such as terra cotta or glass. They may be struck from the outside (101) or by means of a clapper from within (103, 111). Occasionally double bells appear (110, 111), which produce two pitches and may thereby move from the realm of pure rhythm into that of melody and harmony. Bells are frequently employed in liturgical or ceremonial functions. They may also serve as rhythm instruments in ensembles, as charms to be worn, as locating devices worn around the necks of animals, and finally, as signaling instruments. They are found in great abundance in all parts of the world.

Cymbals are concussion instruments made from a round sheet of metal with a central boss. They usually appear in pairs, each pair formed by two cymbals that are matched in size and timbre. For centuries cymbals have been important instruments in the Middle East and in South Asia (125, 127). They appear in all sizes from small finger cymbals (126), to medium-sized ceremonial cymbals (129), to the large cymbals used in the modern symphony orchestra.

Xylophones are *bar* idiophones consisting of tuned slabs of wood suspended over resonators. The pitch of each wooden bar is determined by the thickness of the slab, by the density of the wood and by surface dimensions. Frequently played in ensembles, xylophones are important melodic instruments in Africa (145, 146) and in Southeast Asia (141, 142).

Clappers are concussion instruments in which the sound produced is of extremely short duration. Most clappers are made of wood, such as castanets (161) and shakubyoshi (154). Occasionally jingles are added (151), and in

2. See Erich M. von Hornbostel and Curt Sachs, "Classification of Musical Instruments," trans. Anthony Baines, *Galpin Society Journal* 14 (1961): 3–29.

such a case, the instrument may take on the characteristics of a shaken idiophone.

Idiophonic drums are usually made of wood, frequently in the form of a hollowed log or bamboo tube with a long slit in the top or side. Sometimes of great size, the slit drum is occasionally used to send communications through forests and over wide expanses (174). A smaller type of slit drum is the East Asian prayer-block or temple-block (171).

Shaken idiophones include pellet bells, jingles, rattles, and sistra. Pellet bells are vessel rattles worn by dancers to provide a rhythmic accompaniment to their physical motions, or they can be placed on herd animals and beasts of burden as neck bells to provide and signal for instant location (201, 202). Jingles are small pellet bells or flare bells arranged in clusters so that their surfaces are struck many times in rapid succession by the pellets or by the vessels striking against each other when the instrument is shaken (209). Rattles can consist of seed pods, coconuts filled with pebbles, seed-filled or rock-filled gourds, or any other natural vessel in which some loose material is suspended. They may be vessels equipped with handles (211) or arranged in groups as anklets or wrist rattles (216). Sistra are either frames with sliding rods that rattle when shaken or they have metal disks that slide back and forth on stationary cross-rods. Found in many areas of the Middle East, sistra are of great antiquity (232, 236) and are still in use in the Coptic Church (231).

Plucked idiophones are instruments with metal or wooden tongues that vibrate when plucked. The tongue gives this group of instruments the common designation of *linguaphones*. The most universally encountered linguaphone is the Jew's harp (241), consisting of a metal or bamboo tongue supported by a circular frame; the mouth serves as a resonator, and a melody is produced by emphasizing certain overtones by means of changing the shape and volume of the resonating (mouth) cavity. Another type of linguaphone is the sansa or Kaffir piano (246, 247), consisting of a group of metal tongues supported by a hollow, wooden-box resonator.

The rubbed idiophones are less frequently encountered. The only representative of this category in the Cook Collection is a French nail violin (261), although this classification also includes the musical saw and the glass harmonica.

MEMBRANOPHONES

Membranophones are instruments in which the vibrating medium is a skin or membrane stretched across a frame or opening in a larger body. They may be classified according to shape, materials of construction, or number of heads. Drums, the most common membranophones, are among the most ancient of instruments and are encountered all over the world. They are used to signal, to accompany dancing, and to enhance rituals, ceremonies, and liturgies. Many societies associate the drum with magic and use it to dispel evil, to insure good harvests or good weather, and to promote the general welfare of the community. Drums may be struck with the hands (323, 327, 328), with sticks (315-317), or by pellets attached to the drum by cords (341, 342); they may also be activated by friction.

Drums are perhaps best classified according to the shape of the body. Such a system produces drum descriptions and types such as cylindrical (323, 328), conical (311, 321, 333), barrel drums (351, 354), goblet drums (358), hour-glass drums (342, 345), kettle drums (315, 327, 334), pot drums (332), and frame drums (381).

Small membranes are occasionally stretched across openings in aerophones (523) or idiophones (145) in order to alter the timbre of the instrument. Such devices are referred to as *mirlitons*.

AEROPHONES

Aerophones are instruments in which the vibrating medium is a column of air. This category includes the instruments commonly referred to as *wind instruments*. Aerophones are further categorized according to the method by which the column of air is set in motion.

In trumpets and horns the air enclosed in the tube is caused to vibrate by the player forcing his breath through his lips, which are in turn tightly pressed against a cup-shaped mouthpiece. Western thinking tends to separate trumpets and horns according to shape and bore—trumpets are straight and cylindrical, horns are curved and conical—but in dealing with ethnic instruments where materials that are close at hand or ready-made are adapted as instruments, this distinction is frequently found to be unsatisfactory.

The most primitive forms of horns and trumpets are those made from animal horns, shells, bones, or wooden tubes (441–444). Most of these types operate solely on the principle of overblown harmonics and are designated *natural* horns or trumpets (431–433), although many have been developed to obtain pitches that lie in the gaps of the harmonic series by means of either finger holes (451) or a more sophisticated system of keys or valves plus extra tubing (436).

Owing perhaps to the sheer volume of tone and the ability to sustain long notes, trumpets and horns have been used in many societies as ceremonial instruments and as signaling devices (431, 433). Trumpets frequently serve liturgical functions (421, 425, 426), and occasionally involve pronounced metaphysical and mystical associations (441).

Flutes are instruments in which the sound is produced by directing a stream of air across the sharp edge of a tube or mouth hole. End-blown flutes are sounded by blowing across the sharpened end-edge of a tube. Instruments of this type include panpipes (501), certain kinds of *nay* flutes (504), and Middle Eastern *qawul* flutes (*cf.* 551, 552).

Notched flutes are vertically blown tubes with a rounded or angular v-notch cut into the embouchure (511–517). The facility with which such flutes are made to sound accounts for their popularity in nearly all cultures.

Transverse, or side-blown, flutes have a closed upper end and a side hole with a sharp edge that divides the stream of air and produces the vibration in the tube. Many transverse flutes have a membrane pasted over an opening in the tube to serve as a *mirliton* device, a means of disguising the tone quality. A similar principle is evident in some idiophones (145, 146, 247).

Duct flutes, also known as *flue* or *whistle flutes,* have a narrow duct cut into the stopped upper end. The duct directs the flow of air across a sharp edge cut into the tube. The air passing across this sharp edge sets the column of air in vibration. Of all flute types, duct flutes are the easiest to make sound, and they also appear in many forms all over the world (541–556). In some societies flutes may be played with the nose rather than the mouth; such flutes may be of any of the four main categories already mentioned.

Reed pipes are of several types, usually grouped into single reeds, double reeds, and free reeds. In pipes of single and double reeds, a strip of cane or palm leaf is made to vibrate against a mouthpiece or against another reed, setting a column of air in motion. The length of the column determines the pitch, and the bore, in connection with the construction of the upper end, determines the way in which the instrument "overblows," or sounds upper partials.

Single-reed instruments include clarinets and many far less complicated instruments in which the tube, mouthpiece, and reed are all one piece of wood or bamboo (568). The reed may be cut directly into the tube by cutting three sides of an elongated rectangle, leaving the fourth (a short side) intact. Such reeds may be up-cut (564–568) with the free, vibrating end of the reed away from the tip of the instrument. In such a case the player must "swallow" the reed so that the entire vibrating unit is inside the mouth. Occasionally the reed is enclosed in another vessel that serves the same function as the mouth cavity. In the Indian *pungi* (561), the reed is located at the lower end of a bulbous gourd. By breathing in through the nose while blowing through the gourd with the mouth, an expert player can negotiate a continuous unbroken tone. Bagpipes work on the same principle but facilitate the process mechanically by the use of the air bag. Many single-reed instruments take the form of two pipes bound together side by side. Both tubes may be melody pipes and have finger holes (564, 565), or one may be a melody pipe and the other a drone (561).

Double-reed instruments have columns of air activated by two identical reeds or reed-halves, which vibrate against each other when air is forced between them. This category includes a wide variety of oboelike instruments, bassoons, and some types of bagpipes. Most oboes are of conical bore (573, 574, 578), although some are cylindrical (571).

Free-reed aerophones are instruments that contain a number of reeds of different sizes within an enclosure. The pitch is determined here by the size of the reed, not the size of the enclosure or air column. The free reed consists of a single wooden or metal tongue that passes back and forth through an opening of nearly the same size. Common European instruments that utilize the free-reed principle are the harmonica (mouth harp) and the harmonium (parlor organ), but the free reed is originally an Oriental idea. Mouth organs using the principle are found frequently in East and Southeast Asia (582, 583, 586).

CHORDOPHONES

Chordophones, instruments that have vibrating strings, are usually classified according to general shape and method of playing. The principal categories are zithers, lutes, harps, lyres, and musical bows.

Zithers consist of a neckless body with strings stretched across a flat or nearly flat surface and set parallel to the direction of the longest side. Types of zithers frequently encountered in Africa are those that consist of strings stretched across a hollowed trough (603), across a "raft" of tubes (601), along a single bamboo tube, or along a simple stick. Zithers may be plucked or struck with hammers or sticks, this difference serving to further distinguish zithers from dulcimers. The zithers most famliar to Westerners are the so-called board zithers, which have strings stretched across a more-or-less flat surface. Plucked board zithers include the autoharp and the koto (611). The struck zither, or dulcimer, appears in many parts of the world (621–627), and occurs most familiarly in the form of the Western piano (631, 634).

Lutes are stringed instruments with a resonating body and a neck that extends beyond the body, allowing the strings to be stretched across a greater distance. The neck usually contains one or more surfaces through which tuning pegs are inserted. These instruments may be grouped into long lutes and short lutes, although the distinction is sometimes less than satisfactory for purposes of classification. In general, however, long lutes have necks that are longer than the body, and short lutes have necks shorter than the body.

Classification according to method of playing provides for the further division into plucked lutes and bowed lutes. Each category includes both fretted and unfretted, long and short lutes.

Plucked short lutes can be found all over the world from the Far East (641, 648), to the Middle East (670, 691), and to the European world in which is found the Renaissance lute family and the guitar (693, 694, 697). Plucked long lutes include the *sitar* (665), the *tambur* (669), the *tar* (681, 682), and many others (643, 644, 647, 651, 661).

Bowed lutes, or fiddles, may be either short or long lutes. Short, bowed lutes are thought to have Persian origins and, indeed, they are more frequently found in the Middle East and in Europe than in East Asia and in the Americas. Long, bowed lutes are often called *spike fiddles,* since the long neck usually penetrates the resonance body and often terminates below it in the form of a long spike (731, 732), which in many areas may serve to anchor the instrument in the sand while it is being played.

Bowed lutes may have any number of strings. In some instruments there are strings that are not played, but which sound in sympathy with the other melody strings (714, 717, 732). Bowed lutes may have fingerboards against which the strings may be pressed (743, 745, 747, 749, 750), or their strings may be stopped laterally by the fingernails (707, 717, 731). Some fiddles have drone strings (741, 743, 744), and some have the bow permanently threaded between two strings (707, 708).

Harps are instruments that have an arched or angled arm attached to a resonating body, with strings stretched from the extremity of the arm to the body. A natural arch is formed by the tusk of an elephant, a material used in two harps in the collection (801, 803).

Lyres are harplike instruments consisting of a body with two upward-extending arms and a cross-yoke. The strings are stretched from the yoke to the body, which may be a box or a bowl (811). Lyres were important instruments in ancient Greek culture, where they, along with the larger *kithara*, were associated with the cult of Apollo. The lyre has spread from Persia throughout the Middle East.

DECORATION

In many societies much attention is given to the decoration and ornamentation of all types of musical instruments. Such decoration frequently underscores the ceremonial, metaphysical, or religious importance of certain instruments in particular societies where music may be regarded as a paraphysical connecting link between physical and spiritual realms. For the most part, artistic motifs that appear generally in the decorative traditions of any specific culture are normally carried over into instrument ornamentation, an observation borne out by the decorations on Renaissance and Baroque organ shutters and harpsichords in European art.

Among the most elaborate of decorative practices is that of scene painting, in which the pictorial representation may attempt to include a version of the instrument itself or at least some phase of musical life, or the painting may be purely decorative and ornamental. While the landscapes painted in monochrome on the Japanese koto in the collection (611) are simply ornamental, the polychrome scenes painted on the body of the Persian tar (681) incorporate elements of musical practice in the representations. Furthermore, the landscape scene painted on the lid of the Thai *kim* (623), actually attempts to present in a pictorial scheme the relationship of individual notes of the scale to one another; and there are even stronger metaphysical associations implicit in the brass skulls applied to the Tibetan *bansuri* (546), and in the thunderbolts that decorate both the *bansuri* and the Tibetan *dril-bu* (103).

The lotus flower is a characteristic motif used in the decoration of many Asian instruments, like the ornamentation of the *dril-bu* (103), the Thai *khlui* (543), and the Thai xylophones (141, 142). The chrysanthemum appears on the Japanese temple bell (101), and animal figures are used in the decoration of the Persian grelot (202), the ivory harp from Tanzania (803), several Asian horse-head fiddles (661, 714), the dragonhead trumpet (426), and the Tibetan *dril-bu* (103).

A characteristic decorative motif used in many African instruments is that of the triangle, frequently carved into a wooden surface or "textured" either by cutting or burning parallel ridges close together in the wood (174, 315–317), or by filling the triangle with burned circles (311). Such triangular figures are often part of a larger zigzag pattern (311, 603).

There exists in many societies an apparent compulsion to add decoration to musical instruments. This tendency appears to be strongest in areas where music possesses strong mystical or metaphysical associations and where the visual symbol or the instrument itself may have such associations. It is only natural that instrument makers should discern the close connection between these two types of symbols—music and the visual symbol.

CATALOGUE
OF THE COLLECTION

IDIOPHONES

Struck idiophones

Cat. no.

101* [1] Temple bell. KANE (GYO JI SHO)   Japan

Bronze temple bell struck from outside by a wooden hammer. Rich multicolored patina. Ornamented with figures in relief of four flying creatures and two 16-petal chrysanthemums. Four knobbed panels along top of sides, and two side wing-flanges. Circa 1650.

Collected: Kyoto, Japan, 1965.
H: 24.8 cm (9¾ in); d: 11.9 cm (4⅝ in).

103* Temple bell. DRIL-BU   Tibet

Small metal temple bell with handle and interior clapper. Elaborate lotus and cat's head relief around outside of flare, and lotus figure inside bell at the boss, a motif found in many old Tibetan bells. Handle is in the form of a stylized thunderbolt sculpture. Quilted case also has double thunderbolt attached. Late 19th century.

Collected: Darjeeling, India, 1961.
H: 13.6 cm (5⅜ in).

105 Bell   Iran (Persia)

Small bronze bell with straight flare and missing clapper. Flat perforated top flange for suspending bell. Tarnished surface.

Collected: Tehran, Iran, 1965.
H: 4 cm (1⅝ in); d: 2.2—3.3 cm (⅞—1⅜ in).

106 Bell   Iran (Persia)

Small bronze clapperless bell with graceful concave flare and flat top flange. Pale green patina; corroded rough surface texture.

Collected: Tehran, Iran, 1965.
H: 4.8 cm (2 in); d: 4.2 cm (1⅝ in).

107 Bell   Iran (Persia)

Small flared bronze clapperless bell with three triangles cut out at equal intervals around lower part of flare. Flat perforated top flange for suspending bell. Green patina, rough surface texture.

Collected: Tehran, Iran, 1965.
H: 7 cm (2⅞ in); d: 4.2 cm (1⅝ in).

1. Items marked by an asterisk are illustrated in the section of plates in this catalogue.

110   Double bells   Cameroon

Double metal bells of conical shape fastened together by a u-shaped
brace. Bells are tuned a fourth apart, but each bell is made in two
halves joined together longitudinally such that each bell produces
a double stop. Large bell sounds g# and b′; small bell, c# and e″.

Collected: Douala, Cameroon, 1963.
L: 37.5 cm (14¾ in); W: 22.5 cm (8⅞ in).

111*   Wooden camel bells   Ethiopia

Two wooden camel bells with clappers and elliptical bottom openings. One bell has one clapper; the other has two. Bells are attached
to plaited hemp neck straps. Bells tuned a fourth apart: e and a.

Collected: Addis Ababa, Ethiopia, 1962.
W: 28.5 cm (11¼ in).

125   Finger cymbals. (CROTALS)   Egypt

Pair of bronze finger cymbals. Rough green corroded surface texture.

Collected: Cairo, Egypt, 1963.
d: 5.4 cm (2⅛ in).

126   Finger cymbals (CROTALS)   Egypt

Two pairs of brass finger cymbals, each set tuned a half-step apart.
Modern.

Collected: Cairo, Egypt, 1963.
d: 4.2 cm (1¾ in) and 5.7 cm (2¼ in).

127   Cymbals [SINJ]   Iran (Persia)

Two brass cymbals. Rough corroded surface. From Amlech.

Collected: Tehran, Iran, 1965.
d: 13.1 cm (5⅛ in).

129   Cymbals [ROL-MO; JUMTA; SIL-SIL]   Tibet

Pair of thonged brass cymbals, probably of Indian derivation. Large
central bosses. Cymbals held horizontally like the larger SIL-SNAN;
used liturgically by Tibetan priests. Modern.

Collected: Darjeeling, India, 1961.
d: 16.6 cm (6½ in).

141 ²   Xylophone. RANAT EK   Thailand

Elaborately carved xylophone with 21 thick bamboo slats suspended
by cords over an arched resonating chest that rests on a carved
pedestal. Background and recessed sufaces are red lacquered wood;

2. See frontispiece.

all raised surfaces and sculptured relief are gold leaf. Carvings along both sides and on each end are of rich floral spirals and scrolls of foliage in a symmetrical pattern surrounding a seated Buddha. Shape of resonator is graceful arch. Slats of bamboo are tuned by adding hot pitch to under surface. Part of a matched set (with 142). Modern.

Collected: Bangkok, Thailand, 1961.
L: 124.5 cm (49 in); W: 38.3 cm (15⅛ in); H: 52 cm (20½ in).

142*   Xylophone. RANAT THUM   Thailand

Matching xylophone to RANAT EK (141). Elaborately carved red lacquer and gold leaf xylophone with 17 bamboo slats suspended by cords over a long footed resonating chest. Carved motifs match those of no. 141 with seated Buddha figures and scrolls of foliage on both sides and at each end.

Collected: Bangkok, Thailand, 1961.
L: 128.7 cm (50¾ in); W: 45.2 cm (17⅞ in); H: 40.3 cm (15⅞ in).

145*   Xylophone. BALAFO (BELLAPHON)   Cameroon

Ten-note xylophone with rough wooden slats held in place by hemp lacing. Gourd resonators below slats have thin membrane pasted over round opening—a mirliton device to alter the sound of the instrument. BALAFO is a generic term of xylophones in the regions of Africa located near the Congo basin. Instrument is equipped with a neck strap of dried vine. Early 20th century.

Collected: Doula, Cameroon, 1963.
L: 64 cm (25⅛); W: 39 cm (15⅜ in); H: 31 cm (12¼ in).

146*   Xylophone. MBILA [TIMBILA]   Mozambique

Fifteen-note wooden xylophone with smooth rectangular pine slats suspended by cord lacing on a horizontal wooden frame balanced on two short legs. Each slab has a dried fruit resonator with membrane-covered holes (as in no. 145). Slabs are positioned in groups of two. Such instruments are played as solo instruments as well as in ensembles, even in large "orchestras" by the Chopi who work the mines of Mozambique. Early 20th century.

Collected: Johannesburg, South Africa, 1963.
L: 134 cm (52¾ in); W: 52.5 cm (20⅝ in); H: 23.5 cm (9¼ in).

151   Castanets. CHIPLA   India

Pair of elongated barbell-shaped clappers (castanets) made of dark brown wood with one flat side and one rounded side. Brass rings on the rounded sides permit holding by the thumb and fingers. Twelve metal jingle bells are attached, three at each end of each clapper. Modern.

Collected: Tanjore, India, 1966.
L: 19.7 cm (7¾ in); W: 4.8 cm (2 in).

154   Clappers. SHAKUBYOSHI   Japan

Two long wooden clappers used by the leader of the chorus in Gagaku vocal pieces and used in some temple music. These clappers belonged to one named Hyoshigi, perhaps a Gagaku musician of about 1840. Artist's notes have been written on the sides of the clappers; notation is in Karifu style (See W. Malm, *Japanese Music* [Rutland, Vt.: Tuttle, 1959], p. 263). Pink brocade case.

Collected: Kyoto, Japan, 1966.
L: 36.2 cm (14¼ in).

161   Castanets   Spain

Two pairs of modern black-lacquered wooden finger castanets. Each pair is held together by a red cord.

Collected: Barcelona, Spain, 1962.
L: 8.2 cm (3¼ in); W: 5.8 cm (2¼ in).

171   Temple block. MOKUGYO (MO; MǓ-YǓ).   Japan

Red lacquered wooden temple block (slit drum) carved out of one piece of camphor wood in stylized fish shape with turned wooden beater. Used to mark time while saying prayers or chanting sutras. Occasionally found in the form of a frog or types of fruit, the MOKUGYO is invariably red in color. Modern.

Collected: Philadelphia, Pennsylvania, 1962.
L: 12.7 cm (5 in); W: 10.6 cm (4½ in); H: 11.4 cm (4½ in); stick: 20.2 cm (8 in).

174*   Slit drum   Zambia

Dark brown wooden slit drum (log drum) of trapezoidal shape with grooved triangle designs cut into wood surfaces. Central panel on each side has round wax patch. Two wooden beaters with rough latex heads. Early 20th century.

Collected: Johannesburg, South Africa, 1963.
L: 108.8 cm (42⅞ in); W: 24 cm (9½ in); H: 54.3 cm (21⅜ in).

Shaken idiophones

201*   Pellet bell. GRELOT [CLOCHE; HOCHET]   Egypt

Elliptical pellet bell (vessel rattle). Has two loops in top of vessel for suspending the bell from the neck. Rough green corroded bronze. From vicinity of Kantir.

Collected: Cairo, Egypt, 1961.
L: 16.9 cm (6⅝ in); d: 8 cm (3⅛ in).

202*   Pellet bell. GRELOT [CLOCHE; HOCHET]   Iran (Persia)

Small bronze upright pellet bell (vessel rattle) of elongated globular

shape resting on a four-footed cloverleaf base and surmounted by a
carved figure of a large bird feeding a smaller bird. One pellet is
enclosed in the grelot "cage." Green corroded surface, rough texture.

Collected: Tehran, Iran, 1965.
H: 11.4 cm (4½ in); d: 5.2 cm (2⅛ in).

209   Anklet jingles   Tibet; India

Pair of metal anklet bells (jingles) made from melted coins brought
to India from Tibet by refugees. Modern.

Collected: New Delhi, India, 1961.
d: circa 8 cm (3⅛ in).

211   Rattles   Tanzania

Pair of coconut vessel rattles with wooden handles and small seed
pellets. Pitched a minor third apart. Diagonal zigzag designs cut
into vessel surface.

Collected: Zanzibar, Tanzania, 1963.
L: 21.9 cm (8¼ in); d: 8.6 cm (3⅜ in).

216   Cocoon rattles   South Africa

Anklet rattle made from 36 small moth cocoons sewn to a wide
skin band. Vessels contain small pebbles. Anklet is to be worn by
a dancer, wrapped and tied around ankle. Modern. (*Cf.* P. R. Kirby,
Musical Instruments of South Africa [Johannesburg: University
Press, 1965], plate IVd.)

Collected: Johannesburg, South Africa, 1963.
L: 36 cm (14⅛ in); W: 7.5 cm (5⅞ in).

231*   Sistrum. TSANATSEL [IBA]   Ethiopia

Brass sistrum (shaker) with wooden handle and lattice work along
brass frame. Eight metal disks, four on each of two crossbars,
rattle when the instrument is shaken. Used in the liturgy of the
Coptic Church. Early 19th century.

Collected: Addis Ababa, Ethiopia, 1963.
L: 24.2 cm (9½ in); W: 8.5 cm (3⅜ in); D: 5.5 cm (2¼ in).

232   Sistrum. IBA   Egypt

Closed horseshoe-shaped bronze sistrum from Hermopolis, Middle
Egypt. Tip is decorated with sculpture of seated human figure.
Three hook-shaped crossbars serve as rattles that slide back and
forth when the instrument is shaken.

Collected: Cairo, Egypt, 1961.
L: 17 cm (6¾ in); W: 12.4 cm (4⅞ in).

[31]

236*   Sistrum fragment   Egypt

Fragment of a Naos sistrum of pale, blue green faience mounted on
wooden block pedestal. Side holes appear in the frame to accommodate metal crossbars. Both the three crossbars and rattles are
missing. From east of the Nile Delta (crowns of both Upper and
Lower Egypt appear on base of sistrum).

Collected: Cairo, Egypt, 1963.
H: 16.9 cm (6⅝ in); W: 9.5 cm (3¾ in).

Plucked idiophones

241   Jew's harp. MORSING [MURCHANG; TAMIL]   India

Jew's harp (plucked linguaphone) with circular metal frame and steel
tongue that projects beyond the circle on both sides and curls outward at the playing end. Early 20th century.

Collected: Tanjore, India, 1966.
L: 12.6 cm (5 in).

246*   Kaffir piano. SANSA [MBIRA]   Zaire

Linguaphone with 11 metal tongues and rough brown wood resonator. Circular sound holes cut in top and bottom surfaces of resonating chest. Early 20th century.

Collected: Kinshasa, Zaire, 1963.
L: 36.5 cm (14⅜ in); W: 20.6 cm (8⅛ in); D: 14 cm (5½ in).

247   Kaffir piano. SANSA [MBIRA]   Congo

Linguaphone with 9 metal tongues with buzzing rings (a mirliton
device, see no. 145). Vibrating length of strips of metal is adjustable.
Smooth trapezoidal sound-box of dark brown wood. Modern.

Collected: Paris, France, 1962.
L: 23 cm (8¾ in); W: 9.8 cm (3⅞ in); D: 4 cm (1⅝ in).

Rubbed idiophone

261*   Nail violin. VIOLON DE FER   France
Circular nail violin of mahogany with elaborately carved trefoil
rosette. Pitch of nails is adjusted by driving them further into the
instrument. Sound is obtained by bowing across the nails with a
rosined violin bow. 49 nails and 32 sympathetic strings. Late 18th
century.

Collected: Paris, France, 1962.
d: 39 cm (15⅜ in); depth of box: 7.5 cm (3 in).

MEMBRANOPHONES

311*   Cylindrical drum. CONGA   Zaire

Tall Congo drum. Conical drum with head attached to body by nails driven into body around edge of head. Designs of triangles filled with circular dots are burned into the light-colored wood body near base. Base of drum is cut to form a pedestal. 20th century.

Collected: Kinshasa, Zaire, 1963.
D: 105 cm (41⅜ in); d: 31 cm (12¼ in).

315*   Kettle drum   Mozambique

One of a set of three matching kettle drums from the Shangaan Tribe of Mozambique. Dark brown wood decorated with grooved diamond and triangle designs. Head held in place by wooden dowel tuning pegs. Early 20th century.

Collected: Johannesburg, South Africa, 1963.
D: 29.4 cm (11⅝ in); d: 38.7 cm (15¼ in).

316   Kettle drum   Mozambique

One of two mates to no. 315.

Collected: Johannesburg, South Africa, 1963.
D: 30.4 cm (12 in); d: 38.9 cm (15⅜ in).

317   Kettle drum   Mozambique
One of two mates to no. 315.

Collected: Johannesburg, South Africa, 1963.
D: 34 cm (13⅜ in); d: 39.5 cm (15½ in).

321*   Conical drum   Tanzania

Conical drum with one head held in place by tight close-gut lacing from the head to a ring located at the bottom of the truncated conical resonating body. Modern.

Collected: Zanzibar, Tanzania, 1963.
D: 52.7 cm (20¾ in); d: 21 cm (8¼ in).

323   Cylindrical drum   Nepal

Cylindrical double-headed drum with carrying strap. Heads are held in place by leather thongs in a v lacing. Tuning patch is applied in the form of a large black circle on upper head, small circle on lower head.

Collected: Patan, Nepal, 1965.
D: 38 cm (15 in); d: 13.5 cm (5⅜ in).

327   Kettle drum. BAMYA (BAYA; BANYA)   India

Nickel kettle drum with head stretched over a circular hoop held
taut by leather thongs laced vertically in a w pattern from the head
to a small hoop at the base of the body. Small circular black tuning
patch is applied to head off-center. Played in connection with
TABLA (no. 328). Modern.

Collected: Amritsar, India, 1962.
D: 24 cm (9½ in); d: 25 cm (9⅝ in).

328   Cylindrical drum. TABLA   India

Cylindrical drum of brown wood with head laced vertically by
leather thongs that pass over cylindrical wooden spools that can be
adjusted for tuning to the tonic pitch (*Sa*) of the *raga* being played.
Circular black patch is applied to center of head. Played in connection with BAMYA (no. 327). Modern.

Collected: Amritsar, India, 1962.
D: 24.5 cm (9⅝ in); d: 22 cm (8⅝ in).

331   Kettle drum   Ethiopia

Kettle-shaped drum with camel-skin head attached by intricate
leather lattice work. (*Cf.* M. Powne, *Ethiopian Music: An Introduction* [London: Oxford University Press, 1968], p. 18, Atams, no.s
1687/1705). Modern.

Collected: Addis Ababa, Ethiopia, 1963.
D: 23 cm (9 in); d: 36–39 cm (14¼–15⅜ in).

332   Pot drum   Ethiopia

Chocolate brown pot-shaped drum with smooth dark skin head
attached by leather thongs in an elaborate lacing pattern. Body is
in the shape of a truncated cone.

Collected: Addis Ababa, Ethiopia, 1963.
D: 26 cm (10¼ in); d: 28–31 cm (11–12¼ in).

333   Conical drum   Ethiopia

Tall drum with body in the shape of a truncated cone. Camel-skin
head is attached by leather thongs in a w lacing. Played with the
hands. (*Cf.* kabaro in M. Powne, *Ethiopian Music: An Introduction*
[London: Oxford University Press, 1968], p. 16, no. 1455). Modern.

Collected: Addis Ababa, Ethiopia, 1963.
D: 48.6 cm (19⅛ in); d: 33–35 cm (13–13⅞ in).

334   Bowl drum   Ethiopia

Shallow kettle drum with camel-skin head attached by leather lacing
in a v pattern. (*Cf.* negarit in M. Powne, *Ethiopian Music: An Intro-*

duction [London: Oxford University Press, 1968] p. 13, no. 1753).
Modern.

Collected: Addis Ababa, Ethiopia, 1963.
D: 10 cm (4 in); d: 26 cm (10¼ in).

341*   Double-skull drum. RNGA-CH'UN [CHANG-TU]   Tibet
Double-rattle drum made from two oval wooden bowls joined back
to back and covered with green monkey skin. Two cords of equal
length are attached to the waist of the drum, and pellets on the ends
of the cords strike the drum heads when the instrument is agitated
rapidly back and forth. This type of drum is commonly referred to
as a "skull" drum, since it is frequently made by joining the crowns
of two skulls. Modern.

Collected: Darjeeling, India, 1961.
L: 10.4 cm (4⅛ in); W: 8.7 cm (3⅜ in); D: 6 cm (2⅜ in).

342   Double-skull drum. RNGA-CH'UN [CHANG-TU]   Tibet

Double-wooden-skull drum, similar to but larger than no. 341, with
circular rims covered with monkey skin and equipped with swing-
pellets attached to the waist by two gold cords. A Tibetan beggar's
drum with elaborate gold and pink tassels and streamers. Modern.

Collected: Darjeeling, India, 1961.
D: 10.8 cm (4¼ in); d: 20.5 cm (8⅛ in).

345*   Hour-glass drum. O-TSUZUMI [OKAWA]   Japan
Black lacquer hour-glass drum with two heads stretched across
circular hoops held taut by orange ropes in a v lacing that, when
tightly grasped, alter the pitch of the drum. Used in the Japanese
Noh drama and in the Kabuki theater. Instrument is held on the
player's left thigh and is struck with the right hand. Black lacquer
surface is decorated with figures of trees and flying cranes painted
in gold. Circa 1865.

Collected: Kyoto, Japan, 1965.
D: 28.9 cm (11¾ in); d: 22.7 cm (9 in).

346   Drum: TAIKO (UTA-DAIKO; SHIME-DAIKO)   Japan

Double-headed drum on stand with heads stretched over hoops
placed against a wide black frame. Orange ropes in a v lacing hold
the heads taut (see also no. 345). Used in Noh drama and in Kabuki
theater. Struck in a very small area of one head with a wooden
stick. Modern.

Collected: Kyoto, Japan, 1965.
D: 15.5 cm (6¼ in); d: 34.3 cm (13½ in).

351*   Barrel drum. Small O-DAIKO [TSURI-DAIKO]   Japan

Small O-DAIKO barrel drum. Two heads are held in place by brass
tacks and both are gilded. Black lacquer body has figures of two

goldfish and water plants painted in gold. Two decorated brackets joined to the side of the drum hold brass rings for suspending the drum. The drum normally rests on its side hanging from a stand, but it can be carried in procession by means of the two rings. A form of ceremonial temple drum. Circa 1800-1825.

Collected: Kyoto, Japan, 1965.
D: 20.5 cm (8⅛ in); d: 20 cm (7⅞ in).

354   Barrel drum. Small LAG-NA   Tibet

Small double-headed barrel drum with monkey-skin heads and red, green, and gold decorations painted around the barrel. The drum has rings and loops of cord with tassels for suspending it on a processional pole, or it can be held under the arm and beaten with a sickle-shaped stick. Popularly called "devil dancer's drum," it is commonly utilized in religious and folk ceremonials in Tibet. Early 20th century.

Collected: Darjeeling, India, 1961.
D: 12.5 cm (5 in); d: 25.5 cm (10 in).

358*   Goblet drum. DARABUKA (DARBAKKA)   Tunisia

Goblet-shaped drum made of glazed pottery. Single head is held in place by a light cord lacing around the upper bout of the body. Elaborate black and white geometric designs and figures of running goats are baked into the pottery. Black, white, and beige tassels are attached to the head and to the diamond-shaped lacing. Direction of the decorative goat figures indicate that the drum was meant to be played holding it upside down in one hand and striking it from below with the other. Modern.

Collected: Tripoli, Libya, 1963.
D: 29 cm (11⅜ in); d: 18.2 cm (7⅛ in).

381   Frame drum. UCHIWA-DAIKO   Japan

Tennis-racquet-shaped frame drum with single head stretched across a circular hoop joined to a wooden handle. Prayers are written on both sides of the drum head along with the name and address of the maker. Early 20th century.

Collected: Kyoto, Japan, 1966.
L: 50.4 cm (21¼ in); d: 27.5 cm (10⅞ in).

391   Tambourine   Sri Lanka

Circular brass tambourine with five double jingles. Head missing. Late 19th or early 20th century.

Collected: Kandy, Sri Lanka (Ceylon), 1961.
d: 20 cm (7⅞ in).

AEROPHONES

421*   Trumpet. RAG-DUNG [RGIADUNG; ZANS-DUNG]   Tibet

Long conical straight trumpet of copper and brass made in three
telescoping sections, with elaborate relief decoration on copper
bosses and bell flare. A type of trumpet used by Lhamas for religious
and ceremonial purposes. Usually played in pairs to provide a drone
against which mantras are chanted. The bell end is suspended from
a frame by cords passed through two brass rings attached to the
instrument at the bell, or supported on the shoulder of an assistant.
19th century.

Collected: Darjeeling, India, 1961.
L: 179.7 cm (72¾ in); d at bell: 24 cm (9½ in).

425*   Trumpet   Tibet

Short brass and copper straight natural trumpet in three sections
with a wide, shallow mouthpiece built into the tube, and with a
bell in the shape of a fish head. Conical bore with an elaborate
filigreed boss near the bell. Used liturgically (like no. 421) to play
one note as a drone to chanting, although other notes in the harmonic
series are possible. This type of trumpet frequently exhibits a
dragon's head bell (see no. 426). Various names apply to trumpets of
this type, such as DUNG, DBAN-DUNG, TURYA, TIRUCHIN-
NAM, BUQ, KRIMS-DUNG, LINS-DUNG. Late 18th or early 19th
century.

Collected: Darjeeling, India, 1965.
L: 34 cm (12⅜ in).

426*   Trumpet   North India or Tibet

Short brass and copper straight natural trumpet similar to no. 425,
but with elaborate brass dragon's head bell. Trumpet has conical
bore with cylindrical bell, the two bores separated by a prominent
brass boss. Shallow, cup mouthpiece attached permanently to the
tube. Brass carrying chain. 19th century.

Collected: Zanzibar, Tanzania, 1963.
L: 38.3 cm (15⅛ in).

431   Hunting horn. CORNETA DE CAZA [CORNO DA CACCIA] Spain

Small curved brass natural horn with conical bore and widely flared
bell. Two rings are present on inside edge of curve equipped with
red neck cord for carrying. Mouthpiece lacking. 18th century.

Collected: Madrid, Spain, 1962.
L: 26.5 cm (10½ in).

433   Coach horn [BUSINE; POST-HORN]   United States

Long brass straight natural trumpet with narrow conical bore and
wider conical bell with slight flare at end. Constructed in two
telescoping sections. Reputed to have come from St. Louis, Missouri,
by way of New York State. Used to announce the arrival of commercial coaches. Circa 1840.

Collected: Williamsport, Pennsylvania, 1962.
L: 132 cm (52 in).

436   CORNET [FLUGEL HORN]   United States

Brass cornet with three rotary valves, three crooks, and rummed bell
marked "Klem & Br." Apparently from Klemm and Brother, musical
instrument importers, 275 Market Street, Philadelphia. (See R. A.
Smith, *Philadelphia As It Is in 1852* [Philadelphia, 1852], p. 242)
Circa 1825.

Collected: Northumberland, Pennsylvania, 1965.
L: 35.2 cm (14 in).

441*   Leg-bone trumpet. RKAN-GLING [RKAN-DUNG]   Tibet
Straight natural trumpet made from a hollowed human leg-bone
covered with strips of brown leather and equipped with a leather
loop for carrying. Used by shamans to sound drones for religious
chanting. Strong metaphysical connections exist with regard to leg-
bones, in which the soul is thought to reside. Leg-bones of criminals,
even murderers, are preferred owing to the powerful devils that
reside there. Trumpets made from the human tibia are called
RKAN-GLING; those made from a femur, RKAN-DUNG.

Collected: Darjeeling, India, 1961.
L: 31.2 cm (12¼ in).

443   Animal horn   Ethiopia

Small black side-blown animal's horn. Goat's horn.

Collected: Addis Ababa, Ethiopia, 1963.
L: 16.8 cm (6⅝ in).

444   Animal horn   Uganda

Transverse (side-blown) natural trumpet made from a long graceful
spiral-shaped antelope horn, highly polished and translucent. Oval
embouchure is cut in the side near the tip, which has been shortened
and pierced to provide an additional stop when covered. Light gray
to brown in color. (*Cf.* M. Trowell and K. Wachsmann, *Tribal Crafts
of Uganda* [London: Oxford University Press, 1953], plate 104).
Modern.

Collected: Kampala, Uganda, 1963.
L: 45.8 cm (18 in).

451* Serpent   France

Leather-covered chestnut serpent with six finger holes, metal crook,
and conical bore. Tubing consists of about eight feet of pipe, but
in curved form the instrument extends less than three feet. Finger
holes are placed for convenience of reach and not spaced according
to acoustical principles. Used originally to accompany liturgical
plainsong, the serpent eventually found its way into ensembles
during the Renaissance and Baroque periods. Circa 1785.

Collected: Paris, France, 1962.
L: (without crook) 82 cm (32¼ in).

Flutes

501 Panpipes. RONDADAR [SERINGONASI]   Ecuador

Bamboo panpipes consisting of thirty-seven tubes bound together
in a raft by twine between strips of split cane. Modern.

Collected: Quito, Ecuador, 1964.
W: 45.9 cm (18 in); H: 28.2 cm (11⅛ in).

504* End-blown flute. NAY (NEY; NAI)   Iran

Vertical end-blown cane flute with 5-plus-1 holes and cylindrical
brass tips. Length is divided into five sections by red raffia wound
around the tube. Each section between the wrappings has designs
cut into the cane and stained red. Designs depict musicians, birds,
flowers, and landscapes. Modern.

Collected: Isfahan, Iran, 1961.
L: 49.1 cm (19⅜ in).

511 Notch flute   Uganda

Notched vertical flute made from a tube of yellowish brown unfinished wood. Cylindrical bore with three holes burned into the
front side in the lower half of the tube. Modern.

Collected: Kampala, Uganda, 1963.
L: 50.3 cm (19¾ in).

513 Notch flute. HSIAO   China

Dark reddish brown bamboo notch flute with 5-plus-1 holes and
two vents at lower end. Tube consists of twelve joints of bamboo
that become shorter toward the lower end of the flute. From mainland China. Modern.

Collected: Taipei, Taiwan, 1961.
L: 68 cm (26¾ in).

515*   Notch flute. HSIAO   **China**

Bamboo notch flute of smooth polished bamboo with blue, orange, and green writing and decoration. 5-plus-1 holes plus two vents. One of a set, with no. 525, of two flutes in an elaborate black lacquered case decorated with writing and figures painted in gold. From mainland China. Late 19th or early 20th century.

Collected: Hong Kong, 1961.
L: 64.1 cm (25¼ in).

517   Round-notch flute. SHAKUHACHI   **Japan**

Bamboo flute with rounded notch and hard wood inset in the embouchure. 4-plus-1 holes; slight outward curve (instrument is concave to player). Frequently made in two sections, construction in one piece suggests an older style. Played unaccompanied as a meditative instrument by Buddhist monks and in secular ensembles, such as in combination with the koto (no. 611). Modern.

Collected: Hiroshima, Japan, 1961.
L: 52.5 cm (20⅝ in).

521   Transverse flute. FUE [KOMA-BUE]   **Japan**

Light brown bamboo transverse flute with 7-plus-1 holes. Japanese name seal appears near embouchure. Modern.

Collected: Kyoto, Japan, 1961.
L: 33.9 cm (13⅜ in).

523   Transverse flute. TI   **China**
Bamboo transverse flute of cylindrical bore with 6-plus-1 holes plus one hole covered with a thin paper membrane, a mirliton device. Four vents appear at the lower end. The pipe is wrapped in seventeen places with rings of black thread as decoration and to prevent splitting. Modern.

Collected: Taipei, Taiwan, 1961.
L: 58.1 cm (22⅞ in).

525*   Transverse flute. TI   **China**
Transverse bamboo flute with blue, orange, and green writing and decoration. Mate to no. 515 in black lacquered case. From mainland China. Late 19th or early 20th century.

Collected: Hong Kong, 1961.
L: 64.1 cm (25¼ in).

528   Transverse flute. OTEKI [RYU-TEKI; YOKO FUE]   **Japan**

Transverse flute of dark bamboo with red lacquer around holes and wound with black thread. 7-plus-1 holes. Used in the musical genre Gagaku. Modern.

Collected: Kyoto, Japan, 1965.
L: 38.8 cm (15¼ in).

531 Transverse flute. FIFE — United States

Small transverse cylindrical flute made of metal, with six finger holes and no keys. Late 19th century.

Collected: Philadelphia, Pennsylvania, 1964.
L: 35.7 cm (14 in); d: 1.3 cm (½ in).

541 Duct flute. FUE — Japan

Small whistle flute with six holes. Painted dragon figure on yellow bamboo. Modern.

Collected: Homestead, Florida, 1961.
L: 31.6 cm (12½ in).

543* Duct flute. KHLUI — Thailand

Cylindrical bamboo vertical whistle flute decorated with graceful diamond and triple-leaf figures burned into wood surface and lacquered. 7-plus-2 holes plus two vents near lower end, plus one side hole covered with a thin membrane (a mirliton device) near embouchure (see no. 523). Square-cut flue. Modern.

Collected: Bangkok, Thailand, 1961.
L: 33.7 cm (13¼ in).

546 Duct flute. BANSURI — Tibet

Cylindrical cane whistle flute with six holes, square-cut flue, and beak embouchure. Decorated with small brass ornaments representing skulls, lotus blossoms, and thunderbolts. Modern

Collected: Patan, Nepal, 1961.
L: 39.2 cm (15⅜ in).

547 Twin duct flutes. ALGOJA — India

Two wooden, beaked whistle flutes held together by a cord attached to each pipe at its lower end. Both flutes are played simultaneously, one usually providing a drone for the other (melody) pipe. Each is identical in length, bore, and number of holes (five). Decorated with yellow and green paint on dark brown varnished wood. Square-cut flues. Modern.

Collected: Amritsar, India, 1961.
L: 33 cm (13 in).

551* Duct flute — Turkey

Long vertical whistle flute of dark brown wood with round boss at the lower end. 7-plus-1 holes plus two vents at foot. Usually played in pairs with one flute providing a drone against another melody flute. Decorative rings are cut into the wood surface between holes. (*Cf.* no. 552). Modern.

Collected: Bodrum (Halicarnassus), Turkey, 1962.
L: 76.5 cm (30⅛ in).

552   Duct flute   Turkey

Short vertical whistle flute of light yellowish brown wood with round boss at lower end. 6-plus-1 holes. Usually played in pairs, occasionally in connection with a longer flute such as no. 551 or the QAWUL. Decorative rings are cut in the wood around the pipe between holes. Modern.

Collected: Bodrum (Halicarnassus), Turkey, 1962.
L: 38.3 cm (15 in).

556   Whistle. PITO   Ecuador

Double cane whistle tuned to a major third, used by night watchmen in villages in Ecuador. Bound together by a gaily colored woven band. Modern.

Collected: Quito, Ecuador, 1964.
L: 11.5 cm (4½ in).

Reed aerophones

561*   Snake-charmer's pipe. PUNGI [TIKTIRI; MAHAUAR]   India

Bulbous gourd, metal, and bamboo snake-charmer's double pipe with a single reed concealed in lower end of gourd. The gourd is decorated with brass ornaments, coins, and "jewels." The chanter pipe has 8-plus-1 holes and the drone pipe is a simple metal tube. Pipes are attached to the gourd with wax. Modern.

Collected: from the snake charmer, Benares, India, 1961.
L: 52.5 cm (20½ in); d: gourd 10 cm (4 in).

564   Double pipe. ZUMMARA [YARUL]   Lebanon

Double pipe of cylindrical tubes bound together with black gutta-percha. Six holes are parallel on each pipe. Up-cut single reeds are "swallowed" by the player. A type of double clarinet. Descendant of the ancient SHEM and HALHALLATA. Similar to the MASHURA, SHARGOGITHA, and MASHROQUITA. Modern.

Collected: Jbail (Byblos), Lebanon, 1961.
L: 30.2 cm (11⅞ in).

565*   Double pipe. ZAMAR [ZUMMARA]   Libya

Double pipe of North Africa made from cylindrical bamboo tubes with cow horns attached as bells to the lower ends. Each pipe has five frontal holes directly across from one another. Two detachable up-cut single-reed stems are completely enclosed by the mouth when playing. (*Cf.* no. 564). Modern.

Collected: Tripoli, Libya, 1963.
L: 38.2 cm (15 in).

568   Reed pipe. BALABAN (BALATAN)   Greece

Short rustic single-reed pipe with up-cut reed that is totally enclosed by the player's mouth. Roughly cut red decorations appear on top surface of bamboo. Five frontal holes. Modern.

Collected: Phaestos, Crete. 1962.
L: 22 cm (8⅝ in).

569*   Clarinet in C   United States(?)

Clarinet in C made of light brown boxwood. 7-plus-1 ringless holes and eight brass keys. Maker unknown. Possibly made in the United States by a European-born craftsman. Early 19th century.

Collected: Philadelphia, Pennsylvania, 1964.
L: 57 cm (22½in).

571   Oboe. PIRI   Korea

Simple cylindrical bamboo pipe with 7-plus-1 holes and detachable double reed. Modern.

Collected: Seoul, Korea, 1966.
L: 32.3 cm (12¾ in) including reed.

573*   Oboe. PI CHAVA [PI CHAWAR; PI SHANAI]   Thailand

Double-reed aerophone of a type found throughout India and Southeast Asia. The name suggests possible Javanese origin, but probably the instrument is a descendant of the Arab ZURNA, a double-reed pipe with conical bore that was spread widely by the geographically expanding Moslem culture. The PI CHAVA has a conical bore, as opposed to its cousin the PI NAI which has a cylindrical bore (see no. 571). Made of brown polished wood in two sections, it is decorated with ivory rings along the tube, at the bell flare, and at the mouthpiece tip. A metal circular flange (pirouette) separates the body of the instrument from the player's lips, which rest against the pirouette. Modern.

Collected: Bangkok, Thailand, 1961.
L: 43.4 cm (17⅛ in) without reed.

574 & 575*   Oboes. HARIB (RGYA-GLING) [SURNA]   Tibet

Matching pair of elaborately decorated ceremonial oboes of conical bore with seven finger holes. Each tube is decorated with jeweled brass rings and polished metal bell flares rich with relief decoration.

Two elaborate brass bosses appear near the embouchure along with brass pirouettes (see no. 573). Typical of Asian oboes of the ZURNA type with "swallowed" double reed. Played in pairs. Late 19th century.

Collected: Darjeeling, India, 1961.
L: 62.5 cm (24⅝ in).

578*   Shawm. CHIRIMIA   Spain

Small brown wooden shawm with conical bore and 7-plus-1 holes. Original mouthpiece and pirouette are missing. In their place is a brass ring made to accommodate a modern oboe reed. The tube is decorated with rings cut into the wood surface around the pipe between each hole. Outside surface of tube exhibits neat concave scallop-shape turnings. No bell flare. 19th century.

Collected: Madrid, Spain, 1964.
L: 21.3 cm (8⅜ in) without reed.

Free reeds

582*   Reed mouth organ. SHENG [SHO]   China

Free-reed aerophone in which metal reeds (tongues) vibrate back and forth in an enclosure. Each reed is set in an individual bamboo pipe, and the length of the reed, not the length of the pipe, determines the pitch. Contains sixteen pipes of five different lengths inserted in a hemispheric wind chest equipped with a mouth hole. The reed is activated when a hole in the side of the individual tube is covered. The general shape of the instrument is said to represent the *feng-huang*, or phoenix. It is used to play dense chord clusters in the musical genre Gagaku in Japan where the instrument is called the SHO. From mainland China. Modern.

Collected: Hong Kong, 1961.
H: 42.3 cm (16⅝ in); d: 6.5 cm (2⅝ in).

583   Reed mouth organ. SHENG [SHO]   China

Free-reed aerophone similar to no. 582. Seventeen reeds set in an equal number of pipes inserted in a black wooden bowl. Characteristic phoenix shape. Brown bamboo pipes. Modern.

Collected: Hong Kong, 1966.
H: 48.2 cm (19 in); d: 9.4 cm (3¾ in).

586   Reed mouth organ. KAN (KHAEN; P'HEN)   Thailand

Free-reed aerophone of a type found throughout Southeast Asia, similar to the SHENG (see nos. 582, 583), but consisting of fourteen bamboo tubes of five lengths arranged in two rows and piercing an elongated wind chest. The pipes continue through the wind chest and protrude on the lower side. Sound is activated in the same way as in the SHENG, by covering side holes in the cane pipes. Modern.

Collected: Bangkok, Thailand, 1961.
H: 89.6 cm (35¼ in); W: 12.8 cm (5 in); D: 4.5 cm (1¾ in).

Miscellaneous

599   Statue of double-flute player   Egypt

Limestone carved figure of a seated double-flute or aulos player.

Collected: Cairo, Egypt, 1963.
H: 7.9 cm (3⅛ in).

CHORDOPHONES

Plucked zithers

601   Raft zither   Nigeria

Rectangular cane raft zither of the Hausa peoples consisting of twenty-one narrow tubes of bamboo bound together between split bamboo slats by thin strips of the same cane material. The vibrating medium is thin strips of cane stretched across two bamboo bridges. The fifteen "strings" are grouped in five groups of three strings each. The strings are tuned by wrapping thin strips of cane around them, thereby increasing the density and weight of the string. Modern.

Collected: Johannesburg, South Africa, 1963.
L: 39.3 cm (15½ in); W: 16.8 cm (6⅝ in).

603   Trough zither   Uganda

Tough zither (tray harp) of light ash wood decorated with geometric designs of triangles, diamond figures, and crosses burned into the back of the tray. Zigzag stringing provides for eleven pitches. Tray is of rounded-rectangular shape with a slightly arched back. (*Cf.* M. Trowell and K. Wachsmann, *Tribal Crafts of Uganda* [London: Oxford University Press, 1953], plate 91e). Modern.

Collected: Kampala, Uganda, 1963.
L: 77.4 cm (30½ in); W: 28.9 cm (11¾ in); D: 6 cm (2½ in).

605   Zither   United States

Box zither in stylized pentagonal shape with one right angle. Thirty-one metal strings, dark brown wood with bridge bars of lighter wood. Decorated around circular sound-hole with gold decal design. American eagle and thirty-six-star American flag decal on sound-box. Decal on sound-box with names and location of each note. Marked: Patented May 29, 1894.

Collected: Vicksburg, Pennsylvania, 1958.
L: 51 cm (20 in); W: 29 cm (11¾ in); D: 5.5 cm (2⅛ in).

611*   Board zither. KOTO   Japan

Long board zither with thirteen strings and as many movable
bridges. Close, prominent concentric rings apparent in grain of
wooden sound-board. Other wood surfaces are covered with black
lacquer and painted with scenes in gold along both sides and in foot
cavity. Scroll and leaf pattern is painted along sides of top surface
and at ends. Landscapes and seascapes are painted on sides. Ivory
and tortoise-shell inlay in head and foot. Black lacquered wooden
case with stylized chrysanthemum in gold on top panel (lid). Signed.
Late 19th century.

Collected: Taipei, Taiwan, 1961.
L: 191 cm (75⅛ in); W: 27.2 cm (10¾ in).

613   Board zither. YAKUMO-KOTO (NI-GEN-KIN)   Japan

Arched long board zither ("light cloud" koto) with two strings
pegged frontally. Scale intervals are marked by small inlaid disks
in top surface. Strings are tuned in unison. Instrument rests on long
collapsible stand. Red cords and tassels decorate each end. Modern.

Collected: Kyoto, Japan, 1965.
    : 108 cm (42½ in); W: 11.6 cm (4½ in).

Struck zithers

621*   Dulcimer. SANTUR (SANTOOR, SANTIR)   Kashmir

Trapezoidal dulcimer of reddish wood with twenty-five courses of
four strings each. Bridges divide the strings into one-third and two-
third lengths. Dulcimer rests on a short three-legged stand. Four
star-figures of small punched holes on sound-box serve as sound-
holes. Curved beaters with hatchetlike grips. Late 19th or early 20th
century.

Collected: Srinagar, Kashmir, 1961.
L: 60.4 cm (23¾ in); W: 50.2 cm (19¾ in); D: 14 cm (5½ in); H:
25.5 cm (10 in) including stand; L: short side 33.5 cm (13⅛ in).

623*   Dulcimer. KIM [SANTIR; YANG CH'IN; TAM THAP LUC]
                                                              Thailand

Trapezoidal box dulcimer of a type introduced into the Orient from
the Middle East (see no. 621). Fourteen courses of four strings are
divided alternately in thirds by high bridges. Felt-covered cane
hammers are used to strike the strings. Scalloped and molded sides
of the instrument are lacquered in a brownish maroon color and
painted with gold flowers and leaves. The matching lid contains a
painted landscape with palm trees and seven musicians symbolizing
the different pitches of the scale. Modern.

Collected: Bangkok, Thailand, 1961.
L: 81.2 cm (32 in); W: 32 cm (12⅝ in).

Shallow trapezoidal box zither with molded rosewood case. Thirteen courses of four or five strings each. Two rounded holes with six smaller holes surrounding each serve as sound-holes. Striking hammers are missing. Once in the possession of the Pennsylvania Cameron family, which was prominent following the American Civil War. Simon Cameron was an ambassador to Russia following his term of office as Secretary of War under Abraham Lincoln. It is thought that he collected this dulcimer while on his travels through eastern Europe. (See also no. 631.) 19th century.

Added to the collection, 1961.
L: 116 cm (45¾ in); W: 38.4 cm (15⅛ in); D: 12 cm (4¾ in); short side: 57.5 cm (22⅝ in).

631*   Pianoforte. André Stein, Vienna   Austria

Square pianoforte of light burled veneer with light brown varnish. Two pedals extend from a stretcher below the pedal lyre. Two hexagonal pedestal trunks terminate in a double y-shaped base, each point of the base becoming an underturned scroll foot. Oval brass plaque on fallboard identifies the maker as "André Stein, Augsbourg u. Wien." Range: six octaves (FF to f''''). Obtained by Harold Cook from Mrs. Alda Evans of East Lewisburg, Pennsylvania, who had bought it from relatives of the Cameron family (see no. 627). This piano is reputed to have once been on exhibit in the Pittsburgh Museum, on loan from the Marsh family. Circa 1815. Number 1538 located on underside of case.

Added to the collection, 1962.
L: 170.2 cm (67½ in); W: 80 cm (31½ in); H (excluding rack): 90 cm (35½ in); H (closed): 86.7 cm (34⅛ in).

634*   Pianoforte   United States(?)

Square pianoforte of light colored mahogany. No identification. Support table consists of four simple tapering legs with a rectangular frame at the top. No pedals or knee-swell, but dampers are raised by moving a lever located to the left of the keyboard inside the case. Black and white keys are reversed. Range: five octaves (FF to F'''). Probably American make, possibly before 1800.

Collected: Philadelphia, Pennsylvania, 1964.
L: 164 cm (64⅝ in); W: 57.5 cm (22⅝ in); H (excluding rack): 79.7 cm (31⅜ in).

Plucked lutes

641*   Moon lute. GOGEN (GEKKIN)   Japan

Plucked short lute found in China, Japan, and Southeast Asia. The flat, shallow, circular body gives the instrument the popular name of "moon lute." Light brown porous wood surface along top of body and neck with intricate soapstone reliefs glued to wood on neck and body. Four strings, pegged laterally, are played against a fingerboard with eight wood-and-bone frets. Carved wooden scroll head and tailpiece. The sound-hole is covered with snakeskin. A loose metal flange is enclosed inside the body to serve as a mirliton device. 19th century.

Collected: Kyoto, Japan, 1961.
L: 64.8 cm (25½ in).

643   Long lute. SAN HSIEN [CAI-TAM; SHAMISEN]   China

Long lute with oval body covered with snakeskin on front and back. Three strings are pegged laterally in an open peg-box. Ancestor of the Japanese SHAMISEN (no. 644). Modern.

Collected: Taipei, Taiwan, 1961.
L: 79 cm (31⅛ in).

644   Long lute. SHAMISEN (SAMISEN)   Japan
Long lute with rounded rectangular body covered with goatskin on front and back. Three strings are pegged laterally in an open peg-box that curves backward. Modern.

Collected: Richmond, Virginia, 1961.
L: 98.3 cm (38¾ in).

647   Long lute. TS'ING CH'IN [SHUANG CH'IN]   China

Long lute of modern origin with shallow, flat body in the shape of a hexagonal clover leaf. Three strings are pegged laterally in an open peg-box that terminates in a stylized sunburst medallion. Twelve ivory or bone frets are attached to the neck. Body is of light yellowish brown wood; sides and neck are of dark brown lacquered wood. Modern.

Collected: Kowloon, Hong Kong, 1961.
L: 92 cm (36⅛ in).

648*   Short lute. BIWA [P'I-P'A]   Japan

Short lute with flat almond-shaped body. The back, sides, and neck are all carved out of one piece of wood with a separate belly glued over a hollowed-out area of the body. Two crescents, outlined in ivory, are cut in the surface of the belly to serve as sound-holes. Five strings are pegged laterally in an open peg-box that turns back from the neck. Gapless frets indicate that this biwa is of Chikuzen type. Ivory bridge bar and ivory string eyelets decorate the instrument. Tuned e, B, e F$\#$, b. Modern.

Collected: Kyoto, Japan, 1961.
L: 92.3 cm (36⅜ in); W: 31.5 cm (12⅜ in).

651*   Long ("crocodile") lute. CHAKHÉ (TAKHÉ; CHAKSHAY) Thailand

Long, low, footed tube lute made so as to resemble a crocodile. In fact, its name means "crocodile." A type of instrument that appears in Southeast Asia from about the 14th century. Three gut strings are pegged laterally. Eleven high frets. Tuned A, e, a. Early 20th century.

Collected: Bangkok, Thailand, 1961.
L: 130 cm (51⅛ in); W: 33 cm (13 in): D: 28 cm (11 in) including feet.

661   Long lute. GOPHONG [PI WANG]   Tibet

Long lute with one-piece body of green painted wood and goat-skin belly. Four strings are attached to diamond-shaped pegs inserted laterally in a curved peg-box carved in the form of a horse's head and neck. Sharpened bone pick. Early 20th century.

Collected: Darjeeling, India, 1961.
L: 64 cm (25⅛ in).

665*   Long lute. SITAR   India

Long lute with gourd body, long wooden neck, and ornamental upper gourd on back side of neck. Wide concave neck carries nineteen arched frets that can be moved to adjust to the intervals of a particular *raga*. Two frontal and five lateral pegs tune the seven main strings. Lateral pegs along the neck tune the eleven sympathetic strings that pass over a shorter bridge located closer to the neck than the higher bridge. Elaborately inlaid with bone and ivory, and painted designs of flowers and leaves cut into the bone inlay. Relief work in the form of wooden leaves surround the gourds. Modern.

Collected: Delhi, India, 1961.
L: 124 cm (48¾ in); W: 35.6 cm (14 in).

667   Long lute. TAMBURA (THAMBURA)   India

Small long lute with gourd body and four strings attached to two frontal and two lateral pegs. Rich brown wood elaborately inlaid with bone and ivory and painted with floral and geometric designs in white, black, and brown. Two hexagonal stars made of bone inlay decorate the belly. White tuning beads are attached to the strings below the black bridge. Ribbed, fully arched, gourd sound-box. Tuned c', c", c", g' (an octave above the large TAMBURA), the pitch being only approximate, or altered to conform to the principal insistance tones of the particular *raga*. Modern.

Collected: Tanjore, India, 1966.
L: 61.1 cm (24 in); W: 15 cm (5⅞ in).

669*   Long lute. TAMBUR (TAMBOR) [RABAB]   Afghanistan

Long lute with elongated one-piece body of gray wood. Pointed hemispheric resonance bulb is perforated with small round sound-holes in the instrument's belly. Three main melody strings are attached to frontal pegs, the fourteen sympathetic strings to lateral pegs located along the side of the long neck. The fingerboard is fitted with fifteen movable frets and is decorated, as are also the back of the neck and the body, with inlaid-bone geometrical patterns. Early 20th century.

Collected: Kabul, Afghanistan, 1961.
L: 81 cm (31⅞ in); W: 12 cm (4¾ in).

670*   Short lute. RABAB [REBAB]   Kashmir

Plucked short lute, occasionally (but rarely) bowed, made of yellow-ish pink mulberry wood with rough surface texture. Waisted sound-box is long, narrow, and deep. Gracefully cut neck curves back to form a notched, hatchet-shaped peg-box. Four main gut strings, and eighteen metal sympathetic strings are pegged laterally, the main strings at the peg-box, the sympathetic strings to the side of the body along the upper bout. An ancestor of the SAROD found widely in South Asia. The upper part of the fingerboard is usually fretted, but the part of the fingerboard over the body is left unfretted.

Collected: Srinagar, Kashmir, 1961.
L: 80.5 cm (31⅝ in); W: 18 cm (7⅛ in); D: 21.5 cm (8½ in).

681*   Long lute. TAR (TAAR)   Iran

Long plucked lute with waisted hollow body covered frontally with a thin skin membrane. The body is elaborately painted in many colors with scenes depicting episodes from the Omar Khayam legend, flowers, and leaves. Six metal strings are tuned by lateral pegs in a rectangular peg-box that is also decorated with polychrome painting. Twenty-four movable frets are tied around the bone-rein-forced neck. 19th century.

Collected: Tehran, Iran, 1961.
L: 94.5 cm (37⅛ in); W: 22 cm (8⅝ in); D: 19 cm (7½ in).

682   Long lute. TAR (TAAR)   Iran

Plucked long lute with hemispheric, bowl-shaped body covered with human baby skin. Persian writing appears around the rim of the bowl. Five metal strings are pegged laterally in a rectangular peg-box. Of twenty-four original frets, twenty-one remain. Early 20th century.

Collected: Tehran, Iran, 1961.
L: 80 cm (31½ in); D: 12.5 cm (4⅞ in); d of bowl: 18 cm (7⅛ in).

691*   Short lute. 'UD   Morocco

Short fretless plucked lute with an almond-shaped body that tapers toward the neck, back-turned peg-box, and pointed scroll. Fully arched ribbed sound-box, perforated sound-hole (rosette), and wooden inlaid plectrum protector. Tailpiece is cut in the form of a fan or scallop-shell relief. Elaborate purfling of light and dark wood alternating in an intricate pattern. Four pairs of strings normally tuned G, e, A, d. Late 19th or early 20th century.

Collected: Rabat, Morocco, 1959.
L: 75 cm (29½ in); W: 28.4 cm (11⅛ in); D: 14.5 cm (5¾ in).

693   Mandolin [MANDOLA; MANDORA; MANDOLINO
LOMBARDO] Italy

Small mandola with fully arched ribbed back, wide neck, and sickle-shaped peg-box. Decorated with mother-of-pearl and wood inlay along sides of the back, the peg-box, and near the oval sound-hole. Equipped with six strings pegged laterally and twenty frets. Label inside body reads "Ant. Monzino, Milano/via Rastrelli 10, piano 1ª /Antica e Premiata Fabbrica/di Strumenti Musicali a Corde." Circa 1825.

Collected: Venice, Italy, 1962.
L: 55.7 cm (21⅞ in); W: 22.8 cm (9 in); D: 10.3 cm (4 in).

694   Lute-guitar. LIUTO CHITARRA   Italy

Pearl-shaped guitar with flat back and spatula-shaped peg-board equipped with rear pegs. Six strings, twenty frets. Dark reddish brown varnish. Mother-of-pearl and ebony inlay around sound-hole. Heart-shaped decoration painted on right-hand side of belly. Circa 1800.

Collected: Venice, Italy, 1962.
L: 91 cm (35¾ in); W: 38.5 cm (15⅛ in); D: 11 cm (4⅜ in).

697   Lute-guitar. LAUTENGITARRE   Germany

Modern version of a 19th-century hybrid lute and guitar with fully arched ribbed back, almond-shaped body, and wide fretted neck. Six strings attach to a modern screw mechanism located on the sides of the sickle-shaped scroll with a carved rose relief on the tip. Elaborately carved filigree concave terraced rosette sound-hole. Modern.

Collected: Copenhagen, Denmark, 1959.
L: 94.6 cm (37¼ in); W: 32.5 cm (12¾ in); D: 15 cm (5⅞ in).

Bowed lutes

703   Spike fiddle   Uganda

Tube fiddle with a single string and a sound-box consisting of a hollow ashwood cylinder covered on top by animal skin and left open at the bottom. A long wooden dowel serves as a neck, and the tip is crowned by a tuft of black goat hair. The bow consists of a bent twig equipped with strands of sisal hemp stretched from end to end. From Buganda Province. (*Cf.* M. Trowell and K. Wachsmann, *Tribal Crafts of Uganda* [London: Oxford University Press, 1953], plates 96A, 96E, 115B). Modern.

Collected: Kampala, Uganda, 1963.
L: 47 cm (18½ in); D: 14.8 cm (5¾ in); d of body: 9.8 cm (3⅞ in).

707* Spike fiddle. DAN HO; CAI NI [HU CH'IN] Vietnam

Long-necked spike fiddle with a cylindrical bamboo body covered on the top surface with snakeskin and left open at the bottom, which is covered only by a carved rosette. Two strings, tuned a fifth apart, have the arched bow threaded through them. Two fluted rear pegs penetrate the neck from behind, and a string loop holds the strings near the neck. The scroll is carved in the form of a dragon head. Modern.

Collected: Singapore, 1961.
L: 83.1 cm (32¾ in); D: 12.5 cm (4⅞ in); d of body: 8.5 cm (3⅜ in); bow: 78 cm (30¾ in).

708 Coconut spike fiddle. HU CH'IN [SO-U] China

Long-necked spike fiddle with a hemispheric coconut body and two strings tuned a fifth apart with bow threaded between them (see no. 707). Two rear pegs penetrate the neck, and a loop of string holds the strings near the neck. A type of fiddle found throughout Southeast Asia and China. [SO-U (Laos and Cambodia): DAN HO (Vietnam)]. Modern.

Collected: Singapore, 1961.
L: 71.7 cm (28¼ in); W: 12.5 cm (4⅞ in); D: 9.4 cm (3¾ in); bow: 69.8 cm (27½ in).

711 Fiddle. SHA RANGGI [SARINDA] Nepal

Bowed lute with wooden waisted body and fretless fingerboard. Lower bout is covered with green monkey skin, but the upper bout is left open (see SARINDA, no. 717). The body resembles a shoe in shape, which gives it the popular name "shoe fiddle." The wood body is painted a rose color. Four metal strings pass over a bridge resting on the skin membrane and attach to lateral pegs in a peg-box and scroll turned back at an angle of ninety degrees. The bow consists of a length of straight bamboo equipped with long hairs attached firmly at one end and passing through a hole in the bamboo tube and knotted at the other. Early 20th century.

Collected: Patan, Nepal, 1961.
L: 57.3 cm (22½ in); W: 12.8 cm (5 in); D: 8.2 cm (3¼ in); bow: 36.2 cm (14½ in).

712 Fiddle. SHA RANGGI [SARINDA] Nepal

Dark brown wooden "shoe fiddle" (see no. 711) with short fretless neck and waisted body. Monkey skin covers the lower bout of the body with the upper bout left open. Bamboo and horsehair bow. Four gut strings are tuned by lateral pegs in a peg-box turned back at an angle of thirty degrees. Early 20th century.

Collected: Batgaon, Nepal, 1965.
L: 53 cm (20¾ in); W: 14 cm (5½ in); D: 10.4 cm (4⅛ in); bow: 40.2 cm (15¾ in).

714*   Fiddle. SARANGI   India

Bowed lute with waisted body and square peg-box with three lateral pegs for the main strings. Lateral pegs along the neck tune ten sympathetic strings. Monkey skin covers the belly, and a carved horse head surmounts the peg-box. Early 20th century.

Collected: Amritsar, India, 1961.
L: 52.6 cm (20¾ in).

715   Fiddle. SAREN [CHIKARA]   Kashmir

Bowed lute of northern India with waisted body and large cubical peg-box. The four main strings are attached to lateral pegs in the peg-box, the seven sympathetic strings to lateral pegs along the neck. The belly is covered with brown animal skin. Similar to no. 714 (SARANGI) and nos. 711 and 712 (SHA RANGGI) Modern.

Collected: Shire, Kashmir, 1961.
L: 51.3 cm (20¼ in); W: 7.6 cm (3 in); D: 14 cm (5½ in); bow: 38.6 cm (15⅛ in).

717*   Fiddle. SARINDA   India

Bowed lute with waisted split-gourd body, the lower bout covered with goatskin and the upper bout left open (*Cf*. nos. 711 and 712). Elaborate inlay of bone and wood decorates the neck and pointed spatula-shaped scroll. Three heavy gut strings are tuned c′, f′, g′ by lateral pegs in a semicircular peg-box located behind the spatula. Twelve sympathetic strings that pass through the bridge are tuned by smaller lateral pegs located along the neck. Late 19th century or early 20th century.

Collected: Amritsar, India, 1961.
L: 62.5 cm (24⅝ in); W: 25.5 cm (9⅞ in); D: 24 cm (9½ in).

721*   Bowed long lute. DILRUBA [ESRAR]   Kashmir

Bowed long lute of northern India with a wide neck and arched metal frets similar to those of the SITAR (no. 665), but with waisted, skin-covered rectangular body of the SARANGI (nos. 714 and 715). The body is decorated with painted flowers, and British insignia and lion figures appear on the foot. Four main strings are pegged laterally in a spatula-shaped peg-board; seventeen sympathetic strings are pegged frontally through a wooden strip attached to the neck. Early 20th century.

Collected: Srinagar, Kashmir, 1961.
L: 97 cm (38⅛ in); W: 18.3 cm (7¼ in); D: 13 cm (5⅛ in).

731   Spike fiddle. KAMANJA (KAMANCHE) [SAZ]   Iran
Bowed long-necked lute (spike fiddle) with globular (stylized split-gourd) body covered with a goatskin membrane. The neck terminates in a long metal spike at the lower end and in a turned finial at the upper end. The three gut strings are attached to turned lateral pegs that penetrate a hollowed-out part of the neck. The bow has a white leather strap for tightening the bow hair. (*Cf.* no. 732). Early 20th century.

Collected: Tehran, Iran, 1961.
L: 92.5 cm (36⅜ in); D: 12 cm (4¾ in); d: 15.4 cm (6⅛ in).

732*   Spike fiddle. SAZ [KAMANJA]   Kashmir

Bowed long-necked lute (spike fiddle) with ribbed globular body covered with dark brown animal skin and equipped with a long iron spike at the lower end. A long cylindrical wooden neck penetrates the body and has a turned finial at the upper end. The three main strings are of gut and are attached to lateral pegs at the peg-box, an area hollowed out of the dowel neck. Fourteen sympathetic strings are attached to lateral pegs, seven on each side of the neck. (*Cf.* no. 731). Late 19th century.

Collected: Srinagar, Kashmir, 1961.
L: 107.2 cm (52¼ in); W: 28.2 cm (11⅛ in); D: 24.5 cm (9⅝ in); d: 28.2 cm (11⅛ in).

741   Fiddle. VIALO [LIRA; REBEC]   Yugoslavia

Bowed short lute of yellow wood made in two sections, one of which, the upper part, is darker. Three metal strings run from a tailpiece across an arched bridge to the ends of rear pegs that penetrate a circular peg-disk. Zigzag and triangle patterns are cut into the wood surface and decorate the outer edges of the belly like purfling. The bow hair is tightened by a wooden peg that penetrates the frog of the bow. The middle string normally serves as a drone on the note a′, the outer strings being tuned d″ and e″. Two small circular sound-holes appear in the lower part of the belly. Modern.

Collected: Yugoslavia, 1962.
L: 43.7 cm (17⅛ in); W: 14.8 cm (5⅞ in); D: 5.1 cm (2 in); bow: 35.4 cm (13⅞ in).

743*   Fiddle [LIRA; REBEC]   Greece

Three-stringed bowed lute with waisted one-piece body, raised fingerboard, and f-shaped sound-holes. The strings pass from a triangular tailpiece across a bridge whose foot rests directly on the top of the soundpost, which penetrates one of six small holes in the belly. Nine jingle bells are attached to the bow stick and provide a rhythmic accompaniment. The middle string is normally used as a drone. Tuning: d″, a′, e″. Modern.

Collected: Candia, Crete, 1959.
L: 55.7 cm (21⅞ in); W: 17.3 cm (6¾ in); D: 4.2 cm (1⅝ in); bow: 48.3 cm (19 in).

744* Fiddle. FANDUR [IRA; KAMANJA]   Greece

Three-stringed bowed lute found commonly in the Middle East and in Eastern Europe characterized by a decorated free-standing finger-board, tapering rectangular body, and pointed peg-box. The middle string is a drone; strings are tuned d″, a′, e″. The belly is equipped with stylized c-shaped sound-holes. Frontal pegs. Modern.

Collected: Piraeus, Greece, 1962.
L: 55 cm (21⅝ in); W: 8.2 cm (3¼ in); D: 5.5 cm (2⅛ in).

745 Fiddle [LIRA]   Greece

Three-stringed bowed short-necked lute with a tapering almond-shaped body and flat peg-disk decorated with holes bored into the disk and laurel-leaf patterns cut along the edges of the peg-disk. The belly has two round sound-holes, the sound-post penetrating one of them to support one foot of the bridge. Three metal strings are rear pegged and are usually tuned d″, a′, e″. Middle string is normally employed as a drone. Modern.

Collected: Rhodes, 1962.
L: 40.6 cm (16 in); W: 13 cm (5⅛ in); D: 5 cm (2 in).

746 Fiddle [LIRA]   Greece

Four-stringed bowed long-necked lute of the LIRA type with a two-piece almond-shaped body and flat spatula peg-board equipped with rear pegs. Clear yellow varnished pine. Strings might be tuned in the so-called Turkish tuning (G, d, a, e″) or modified to the modern European violin tuning (g, d′, a′, e″). Modern.

Collected: Rhodes, 1962.
L: 51.3 cm (20⅛ in); W: 13.5 cm (5¼ in); D: 7.7 cm (3 in); bow: 44.3 cm (17⅜ in).

747 Fiddle   Turkey

Bowed short-necked lute with waisted body of light yellow brown unfinished wood. Similar to the Greek folk LIRA (nos. 743 and 745) in that the bridge rests on the sound-post that penetrates one of two s-shaped sound-holes in the belly. Four metal strings are attached to lateral pegs in a peg-box turned back at a forty-five degree angle and surmounted by a primitive carving of a turtle head. This instru-ment represents a modern mutation of the European violin and the folk lira. Modern.

[55]

Collected: Rhodes, 1962.
L: 43.5 cm (17⅛ in); W: 12.2 cm (4¾ in); bow: 44 cm (17⅜ in).

749   Fiddle   Iran

Bowed short-necked lute with fretless fingerboard that combines
features of the European violin and the Persian TAR (see no. 681).
Similar to the violin in size and shape, but equipped with two round
openings on the belly covered with a thin opaque skin membrane.
The bridge rests on the lower skin, and the upper skin is stretched
across an area under the free fingerboard. The fiddle has a heavy,
humpbacked body with a violin scroll equipped with four lateral
pegs. Tuned g, d′, a′, e″. Painted dark brown. Late 19th century.

Collected: Tehran, Iran, 1966.
L: 57.8 cm (22¾ in); W: 17.5 cm (6⅞ in); D: 12.6 cm (5 in).

750°   Dancing master's fiddle. POCHE [KIT; REBEC]   Italy

Small narrow bowed short-necked lute with sickle-shaped peg-box
and fluted arched back. Called POCHE because it could be carried
about easily in a pocket. Traditionally carried by dancing teachers,
it was much in vogue in the latter half of the 18th century. The
instrument is outfitted like the violin, but has a long narrow body.
Tuned like the violin, g, d′, a′, e″. Light brown wood with black
and white purfling. Made by Carlo de March, Venice. Modern.

Collected: Venice, Italy, 1962.
L: 48.3 cm (19 in).

761°   Hurdy-gurdy. VIÈLLE À ROUE   France

Elaborately painted and inlaid hurdy-gurdy with lute-shaped body
and six strings attached by frontal pegs. The scroll is carved in the
form of a maiden's face and head and is painted in many colors. The
strings are activated by a wheel covered with rosin dust, which is
turned by a crank mechanism at the foot of the instrument. The
melody string is fretted by a mechanism of twenty-three black-and-
white keys. Five strings are drones. The body is decorated with a
flower-and-leaf design painted on the mechanism lid and wheel lid.
Two types of wood and mother-of-pearl make up the inlaid purfling.
Neatly cut c-shaped sound-holes appear near the lower end of the
belly. The back is ribbed and fully arched. Colored ribbons and
streamers are attached to the neck. Label reads, "Pajot, fils, a Jenzat
par Gannot (Allier)." Late 18th century.

Collected: Berry, France, 1959.
L: 73 cm (28¾ in); W: 31.6 cm (12⅜ in); D: 25.2 cm (9⅞ in).

Harps and lyres

801   Harp   Zaire

Arched ivory harp with cobra-skin covering applied to the elongated oval resonating body. The arm of the harp is an ivory tusk with a human head carved at the tip. The cobra skin has circular sound-holes cut into the surface. Four hemp strings. Modern.

Collected: Madrid, Spain, 1962.
H: 57 cm (22½ in); W: 10.5 cm (4⅛ in).

803*   Harp   Tanzania

Arched ivory harp with horsehair-covered resonating body of pointed oval shape. Five hemp strings extend from the body to ebony pegs that laterally pierce the upper part of the arm. The arm is an elaborately carved ivory tusk, with carvings representing a crocodile swallowing a man who is in turn holding a basket over his head with two more crocodiles above, their tails forming the pointed tip of the arm. From Tanganyika. Early 20th century.

Collected: Mombasa, Kenya, 1963.
H: 82.8 cm (32½ in); W: 22 cm (8⅝ in).

807*   Harp   Uganda

Arched wooden harp with rectangular sound-box whose top is covered with brown leather nailed to the box around the edges. Straight-line designs are burned into the sides and back of the body, and two circular holes cut in the leather covering serve as sound-holes. The arched arm contains five lateral pegs to which are attached metal strings. Obtained from Pygmies near Bundibugyo, Uganda, who may have brought it from the Congo.

Collected: near Bundibugyo, Uganda, 1963.
L: 54 cm (21¼ in); W: 10.3 cm (5⅛ in); D: 5.6 cm (2¼ in).

811*   Lyre. KISSAR   Sudan

Bowl lyre with cane arms and yoke, decorated with strands of tiny colored beads and clumps of black sheep's wool wrapped around the triangular yoke. Six gut strings pass over a wooden bridge located between two circular sound-holes cut into the sheepskin membrane that covers the bowl. From the Nubian Desert. Modern.

Collected: Cairo, Egypt, 1961.
H: 89 cm (35 in); W: 65 cm (25½ in); D: 11.5 cm (4½ in); d of bowl: 36.5 cm (14⅜ in).

MISCELLANEOUS

999   Dancer's skirt   Swaziland

Dancer's skirt of straw consisting of a wide belt with straw tassels, common in southern Africa.

Collected: Golel, Swaziland, 1963.
L: 27 cm (10⅝ in); waist: 98 cm (38½ in).

Selected Bibliography

Baines, Anthony, ed. *Musical Instruments through the Ages*. London: Pelican Books, 1961.

Bragard, Roger, and De Hen, Ferdinand. *Musical Instruments in Art and History*. Translated by Bill Hopkins. New York: Viking, 1968.

Buchner, Alexander. *Folk Music Instruments of the World*. New York: Crown, 1972.

————— *Musical Instruments through the Ages*. Translated by Iris Urwin. London: Spring Books [1956].

Chao-Mei-Pa. *The Yellow Bell: A Brief Sketch of the History of Chinese Music*. Baldwin, Md.: Barberry Hill, 1934.

Crossley-Holland, Peter. "The Religious Music of Tibet and Its Cultural Background." In *Proceedings of the Centennial Workshop on Ethnomusicology, Vancouver, 1967*. Vancouver: University of British Columbia, 1968, pp. 79–91.

Danielou, Alain. *La musique de Cambodge et du Laos*. Pondichéry: Institut Français d'Indologie, 1957.

Engel, Carl. *The Music of the Most Ancient Nations*. London: William Reeves, 1929.

Grove's Dictionary of Music and Musicians. 5th ed. London: Macmillan, 1954.

Hood, Mantle. *The Ethnomusicologist*. New York: McGraw-Hill, 1971.

Hornbostel, Erich M. von, and Sachs, Curt. "Classification of Musical Instruments." Translated by Anthony Baines and Klaus P. Wachsmann. *Galpin Society Journal* 14 (1961): 3–29.

Jenkins, Jean L. *Musical Instruments. Horniman Museum, London*. 2nd ed. London: Inner London Education Authority, 1970.

—————, ed. *Ethnic Musical Instruments: Identification—Conservation*. London: Hugh Evelyn for the International Council of Museums, 1970.

Kirby, Percival R. *The Musical Instruments of the Native Races of South Africa.* 2nd ed. Johannesburg: Witwatersrand University Press, 1965.

Kishibe, Shigeo. *The Traditional Music of Japan.* Tokyo: Japan Cultural Society, 1969.

Kothari, K. S. *Indian Folk Musical Instruments.* New Delhi: Sangeet Notak Akademi, 1968.

Kunst, Jaap. *Hindu-Javanese Musical Instruments.* The Hague: Martinus Nijhoff, 1968.

Liang, Tsai-Ping. *Chinese Musical Instruments and Pictures.* Taipei: Chinese Classical Music Association, 1970.

Malm, William P. *Japanese Music and Musical Instruments.* Rutland, Vt.: Tuttle, 1959.

———— *Music Cultures of the Pacific, the Near East, and Asia.* Englewood Cliffs, N. J.: Prentice Hall, 1967.

Marcuse, Sibyl. *Musical Instruments: A Comprehensive Dictionary.* Garden City, N. Y.: Doubleday, 1964.

Miller, Lloyd. "Music of the East." Syllabus for Music 327, Division of Continuing Education Correspondence Study. Reproduced typescript. Salt Lake City, Utah: University of Utah, 1970.

———— "A Survey of Oriental Music." Reproduced typescript. Salt Lake City, Utah: University of Utah, 1968.

Die Musik in Geschichte und Gegenwart. Kassel: Barenreiter, 1949–1968.

Nettl, Bruno. *Folk and Traditional Music of the Western Continents.* Englewood Cliffs, N. J.: Prentice Hall, 1965.

———— *Theory and Method in Ethnomusicology.* London: Free Press of Glencoe, Collier-Macmillan, 1964.

Powne, Michael. *Ethiopian Music: An Introduction.* London: Oxford University Press, 1968.

Rimmer, Joan. *Ancient Musical Instruments of Western Asia in the Department of Western Asiatic Antiquities, The British Museum.* London: The British Museum, 1969.

Russell, Raymond, and Baines, Anthony. *Catalogue of Musical Instruments. Victoria and Albert Museum.* London: H.M. Stationery Office, 1968.

Sachs, Curt. *Handbuch der Instrumentenkunde.* Hildesheim: Georg Olms Verlag, 1971.

———— *The History of Musical Instruments.* New York: W. W. Norton, 1940.

———— *Reallexikon der Musikinstrumente.* Hildesheim: Georg Olms Verlag, 1962.

Schaeffner, André. *Origine des instruments de musique.* Reprint ed. Paris: Mouton, 1968.

Slobin, Mark. *Kirgiz Instrumental Music.* New York: Society for Asian Music, 1969.

Tran Van Khe. *La musique vietnamienne traditionnelle.* Paris: Presses Universitaires, 1962.

Trowell, Margaret, and Wachsmann, Klaus P. *Tribal Crafts of Uganda.* London: Oxford University Press, 1953.

Wachsmann, Klaus P., ed. *Essays on Music and History in Africa.* Evanston, Illinois: Northwestern University Press, 1971.

List of Instruments in Collection

<table>
<tr><td>Catalogue No.</td><td>Catalogue No.</td></tr>
<tr><td>101 Temple bell (Japan)</td><td>232 Sistrum (Egypt)</td></tr>
<tr><td>103 Temple bell (Tibet)</td><td>236 Sistrum fragment (Egypt)</td></tr>
<tr><td>105 Bell (Iran)</td><td>241 Jew's harp (India)</td></tr>
<tr><td>106 Bell (Iran)</td><td>246 Sansa (Zaire)</td></tr>
<tr><td>107 Bell (Iran)</td><td>247 Sansa (Congo)</td></tr>
<tr><td>110 Cow bells (Cameroon)</td><td>261 Nail violin (France)</td></tr>
<tr><td>111 Camel bells (Ethiopia)</td><td>311 Congo drum (Zaire)</td></tr>
<tr><td>125 Cymbals (Egypt)</td><td>315 Kettle drum (Mozambique)</td></tr>
<tr><td>126 Finger cymbals (Egypt)</td><td>316 Kettle drum (Mozambique)</td></tr>
<tr><td>127 Cymbals (Iran)</td><td>317 Kettle drum (Mozambique)</td></tr>
<tr><td>129 Cymbals (Tibet)</td><td>321 Conical drum (Tanzania)</td></tr>
<tr><td>141 Xylophone (Thailand)</td><td>323 Cylindrical drum (Nepal)</td></tr>
<tr><td>142 Xylophone (Thailand)</td><td>327 Kettle drum (India)</td></tr>
<tr><td>145 Xylophone (Cameroon)</td><td>328 Cylindrical drum (India)</td></tr>
<tr><td>146 Xylophone (Mozambique)</td><td>331 Kettle drum (Ethiopia)</td></tr>
<tr><td>151 Castanets (India)</td><td>332 Pot drum (Ethiopia)</td></tr>
<tr><td>154 Clappers (Japan)</td><td>333 Conical drum (Ethiopia)</td></tr>
<tr><td>161 Castanets (Spain)</td><td>334 Kettle drum (Ethiopia)</td></tr>
<tr><td>171 Temple block (Japan)</td><td>341 Skull drum (Tibet)</td></tr>
<tr><td>174 Slit drum (South Africa)</td><td>342 Skull drum (Tibet)</td></tr>
<tr><td>201 Pellet bell (Egypt)</td><td>345 Hour-glass drum (Japan)</td></tr>
<tr><td>202 Pellet bell (Iran)</td><td>346 Shallow drum (Japan)</td></tr>
<tr><td>209 Anklet jingles (India)</td><td>351 Barrel drum (Japan)</td></tr>
<tr><td>211 Coconut rattles (Tanzania)</td><td>354 Barrel drum (Tibet)</td></tr>
<tr><td>216 Cocoon rattle (South Africa)</td><td>358 Goblet drum (Tunisia)</td></tr>
<tr><td>231 Sistrum (Ethiopia)</td><td>381 Frame drum (Japan)</td></tr>
</table>

391	Tambourine (Sri Lanka)		621	Dulcimer (Kashmir)
421	Horn (Tibet)		623	Dulcimer (Thailand)
425	Trumpet (Tibet)		627	Dulcimer (United States)
426	Trumpet (India)		631	Pianoforte (Austria)
431	Hunting horn (Spain)		634	Pianoforte (United States?)
433	Coach horn (United States)		641	Short lute (Japan)
436	Cornet (United States)		643	Long lute (China)
441	Leg-bone trumpet (Tibet)		644	Long lute (Japan)
443	Animal's horn (Ethiopia)		647	Long lute (China)
444	Antelope horn (Uganda)		648	Long lute (Japan)
451	Serpent (France)		651	Crocodile lute (Thailand)
501	Panpipes (Ecuador)		661	Long lute (Tibet)
504	End-blown flute (Iran)		665	Long lute (India)
511	Notch flute (Uganda)		667	Long lute (India)
513	Notch flute (China)		669	Long lute (Afghanistan)
515	Notch flute (China)		670	Short lute (Kashmir)
517	Notch flute (Japan)		681	Long lute (Iran)
521	Transverse flute (Japan)		682	Long lute (Iran)
523	Transverse flute (China)		691	Short lute (Morocco)
525	Transverse flute (China)		693	Short lute (Italy)
528	Transverse flute (Japan)		694	Lute-guitar (Italy)
531	Fife (United States)		697	Lute-guitar (Germany)
541	Whistle flute (Japan)		703	Spike fiddle (Uganda)
543	Whistle flute (Thailand)		707	Spike fiddle (China)
546	Whistle flute (Tibet)		708	Spike fiddle (China)
547	Double flute (India)		711	Fiddle (Nepal)
551	Whistle flute (Turkey)		712	Fiddle (Nepal)
552	Whistle flute (Turkey)		714	Fiddle (India)
556	Double flute (Ecuador)		715	Fiddle (Kashmir)
561	Snake-charmer's pipe (India)		717	Fiddle (India)
564	Double clarinet (Lebanon)		721	Fiddle (Kashmir)
565	Double clarinet (Libya)		731	Spike fiddle (Iran)
568	Clarinet (Greece)		732	Spike fiddle (Kashmir)
569	Clarinet (United States?)		741	Fiddle (Yugoslavia)
571	Oboe (Korea)		743	Fiddle (Greece)
573	Oboe (Thailand)		744	Fiddle (Greece)
574	Oboe (Tibet)		745	Fiddle (Greece)
575	Oboe (Tibet)		746	Fiddle (Greece)
578	Shawm (Spain)		747	Fiddle (Turkey)
582	Mouth organ (China)		749	Fiddle (Iran)
583	Mouth organ (China)		750	Dancing master's fiddle (Italy)
586	Mouth organ (Thailand)		761	Hurdy-gurdy (France)
601	Raft zither (South Africa)		801	Harp (Zaire)
603	Trough zither (Uganda)		803	Harp (Tanzania)
605	Zither (United States)		807	Harp (Uganda)
611	Zither (Japan)		811	Bowl lyre (Sudan)
613	Zither (Japan)		999	Grass skirt (Swaziland)

Index of Instruments by Country
(Numbers refer to catalogue entry)

Index
(Bold face numbers refer to catalogue entry)

PLATES

101. Temple Bell, Japan

103. Temple Bell, Tibet

111.   Camel Bells, Ethiopia

146.   Xylophone, Mozambique

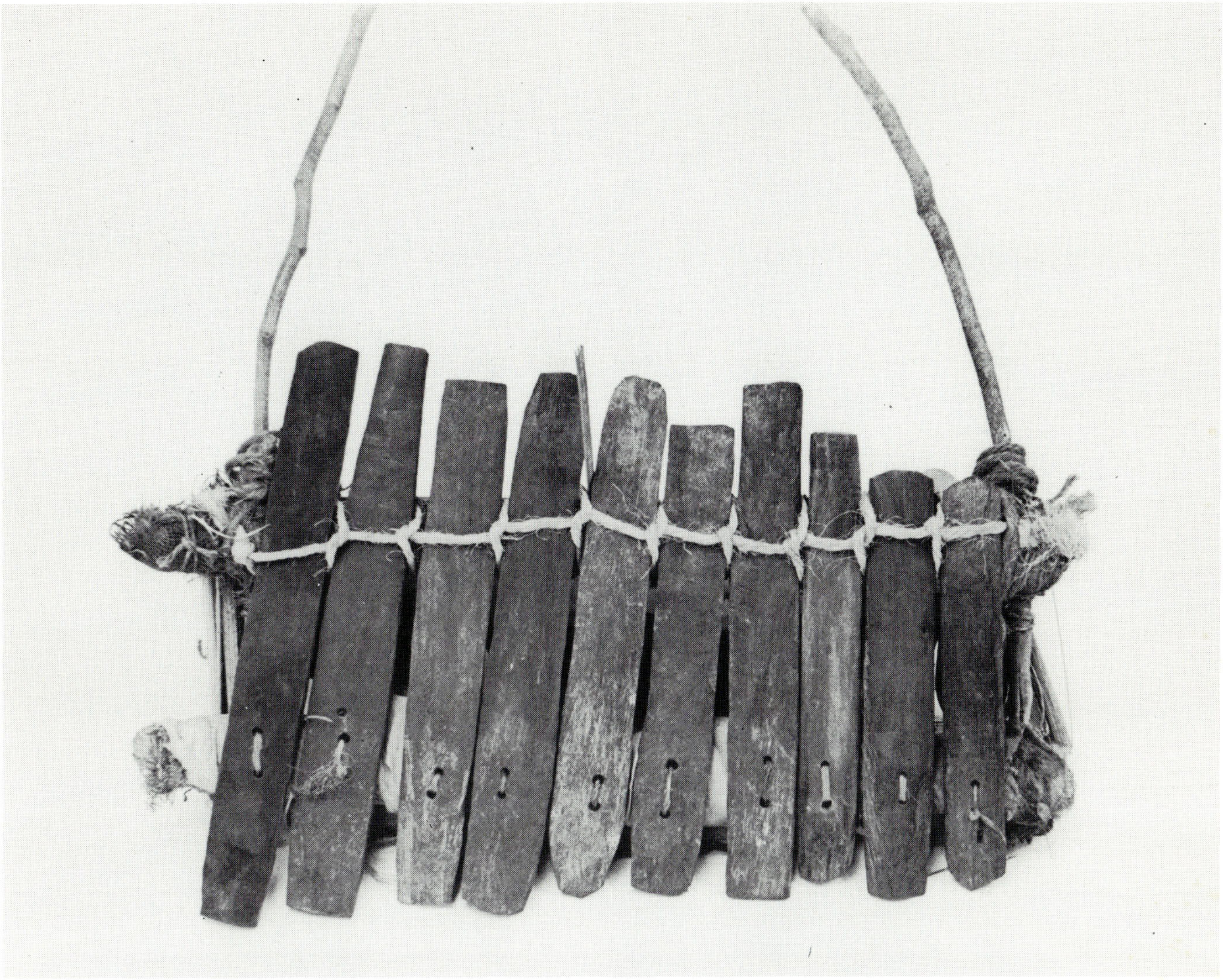

145.   Xylophone, Cameroon

174.   Slit Drum, South Africa

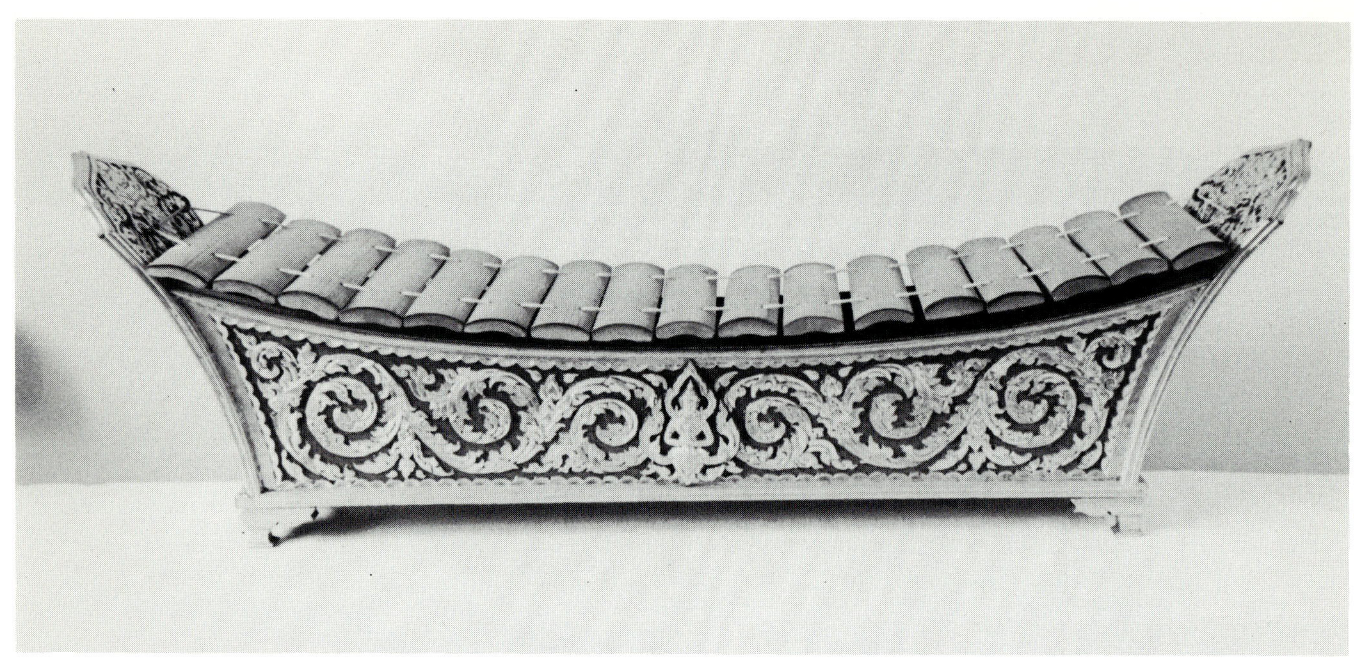

142.   Xylophone, Thailand

141.   Detail of Xylophone, Thailand

201.   Grelot, Egypt

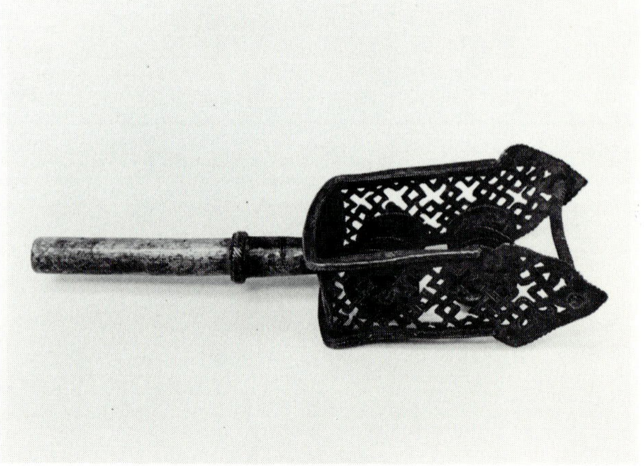

231.   Sistrum, Ethiopia

202.   Grelot, Iran

236.   Sistrum, Egypt

246.   Sansa, Congo

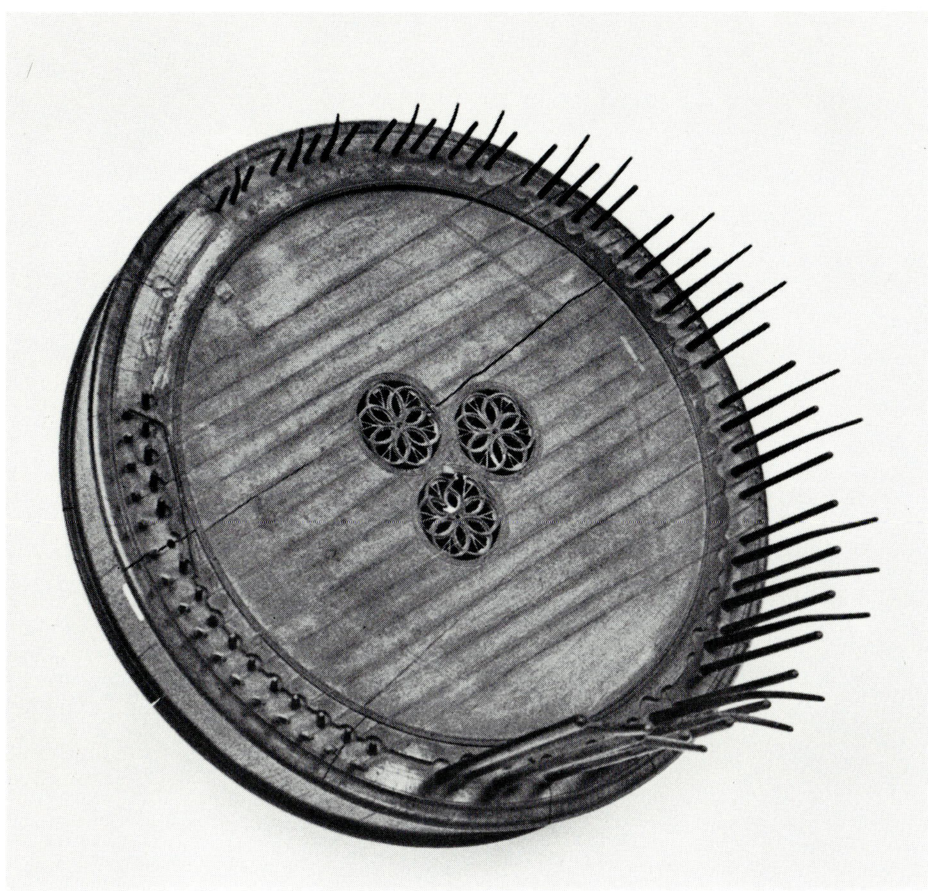

261.   Nail Violin, France

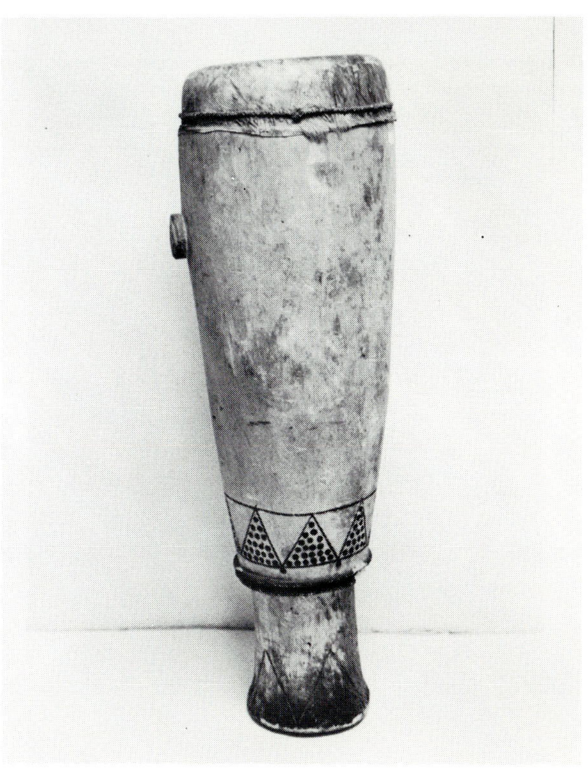

311.   Drum, Congo

345.   Hour-glass Drum, Japan

321.   Drum, Tanzania

358.　Goblet Drum, Tunisia

315. Kettle Drum, Mozambique

341. Skull Drum, Tibet

351. Barrel Drum, Japan

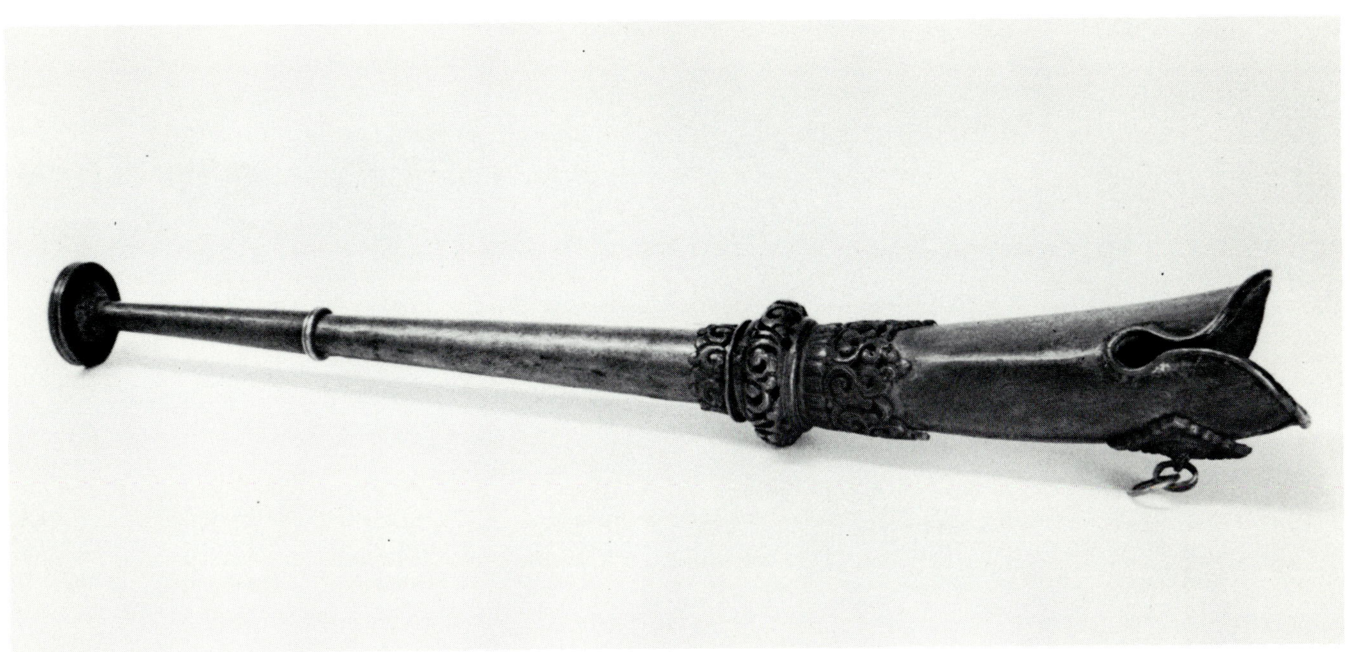

425.   Trumpet, Tibet

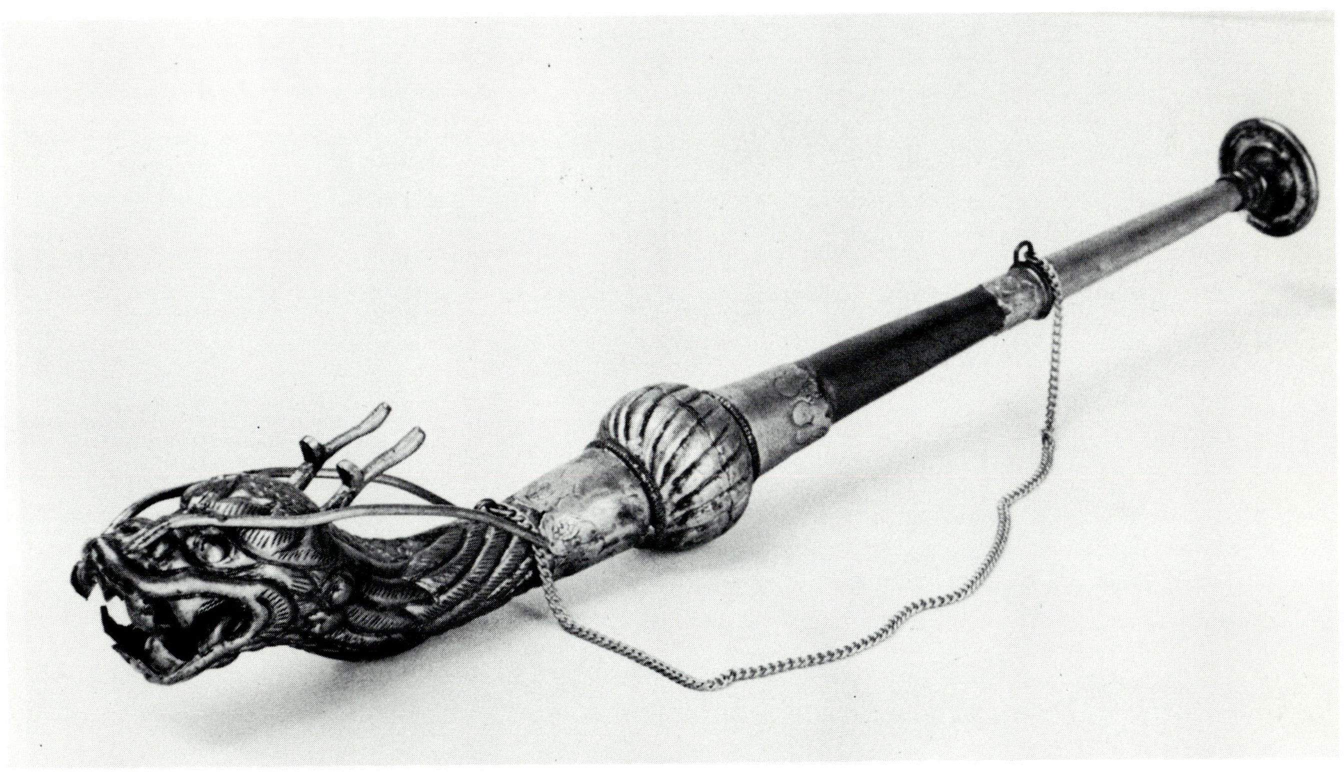

426.   Trumpet, Tibet or North India

451.   Serpent, France

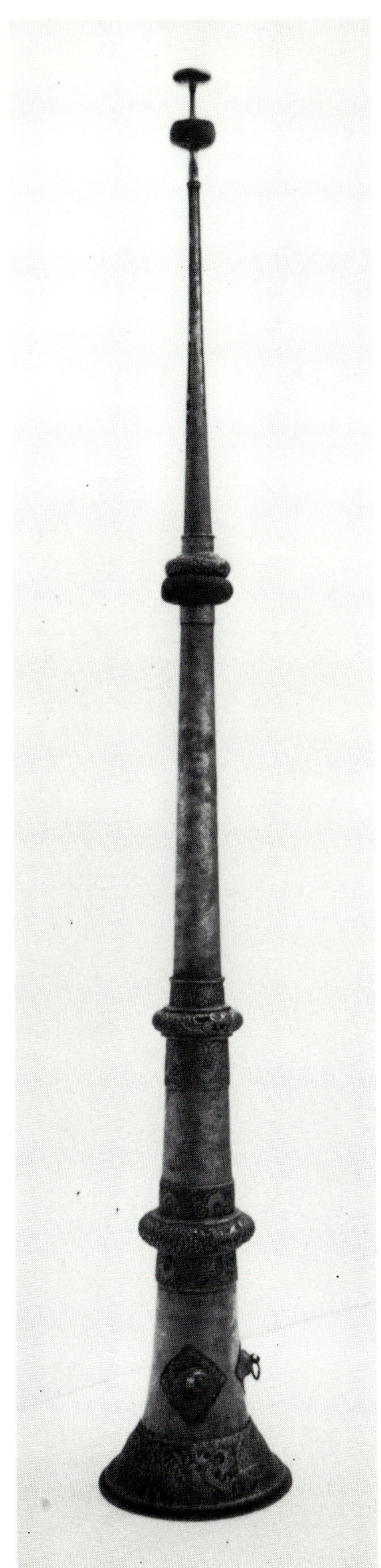

421.   Trumpet, Tibet

441.   Leg-bone Trumpet, Tibet

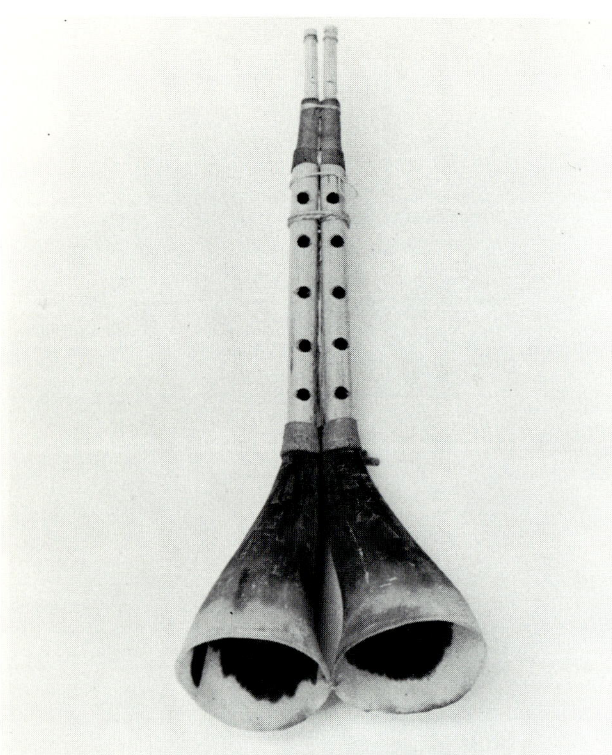

565. Double Pipe, Libya

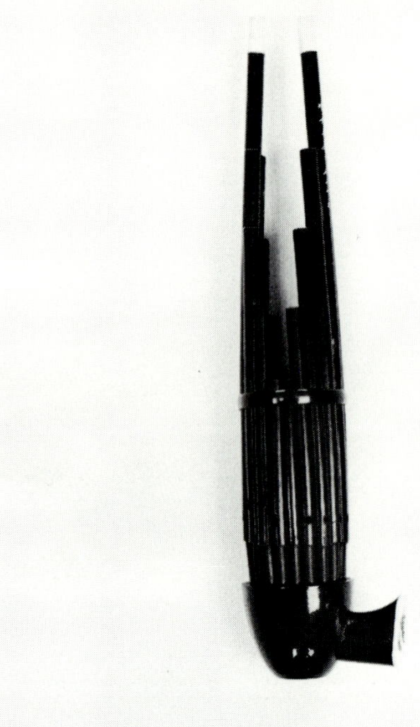

582. Mouth Organ, China

561. Snake-charmer's Pipe, India

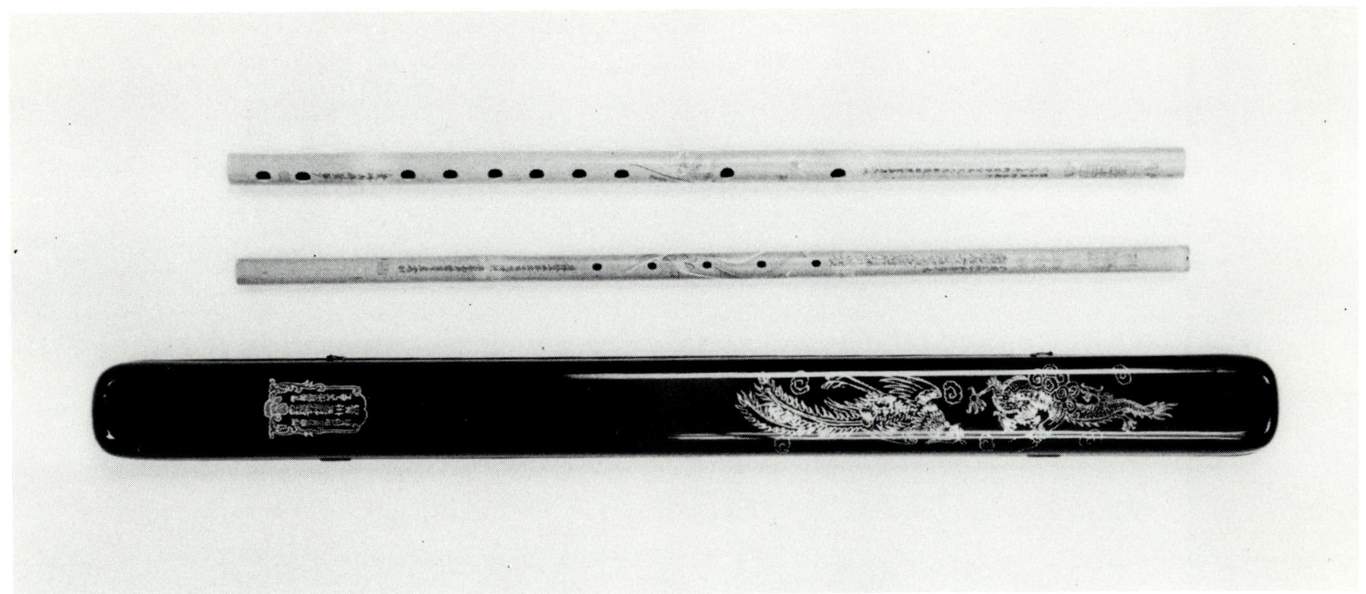

515 & 525.   Flutes and Case, China

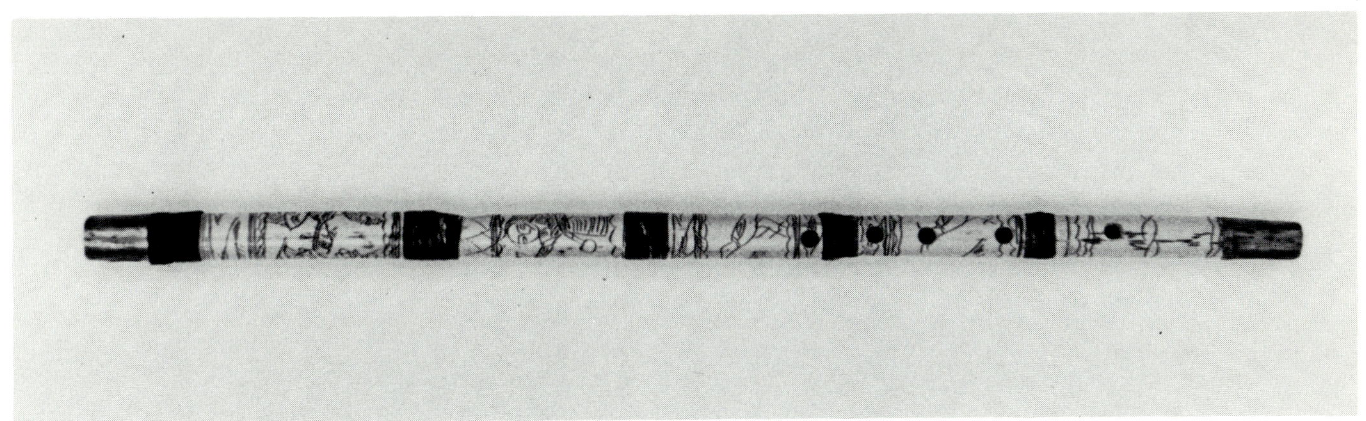

504.   End-blown Flute, Iran

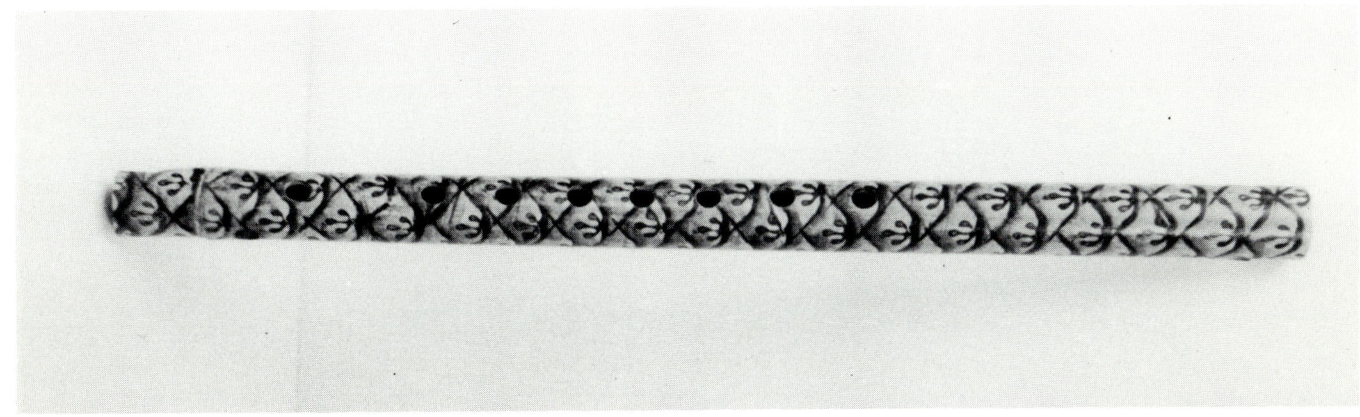

543.   Duct Flute, Thailand

551. Duct Flute, Turkey

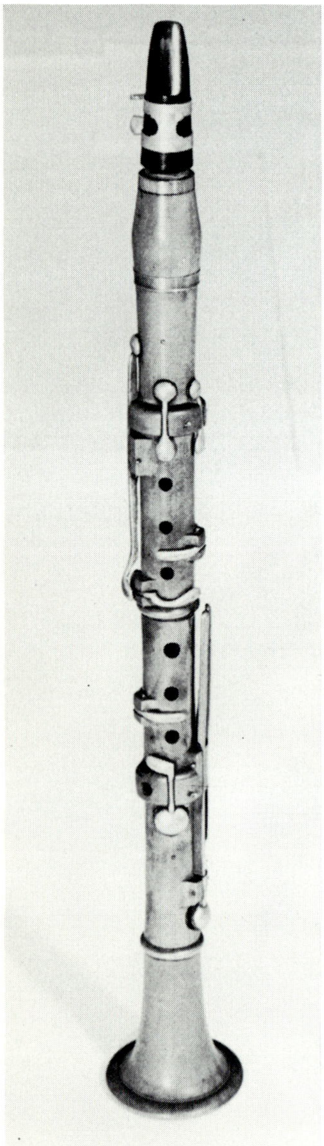

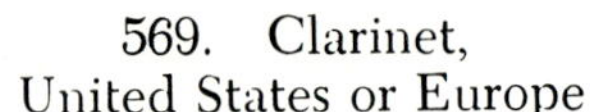

569. Clarinet,
United States or Europe

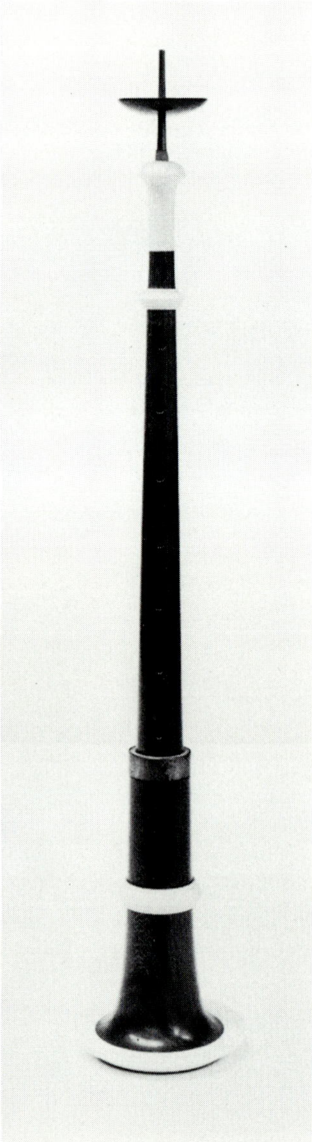

573. Oboe, Thailand

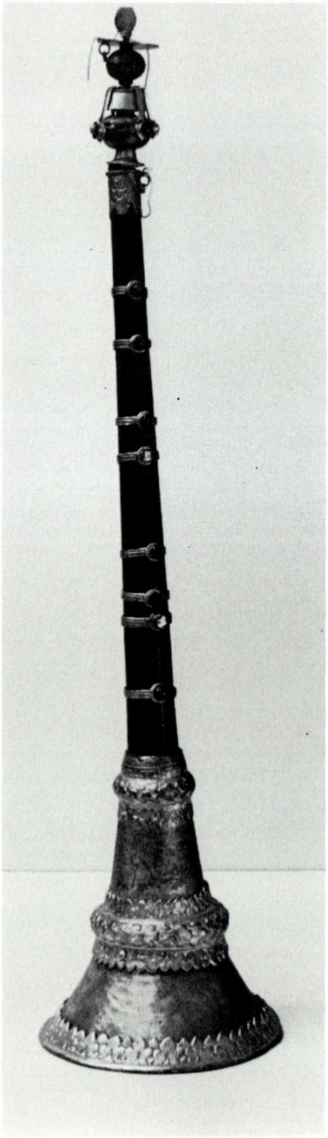

574. Oboe, Tibet

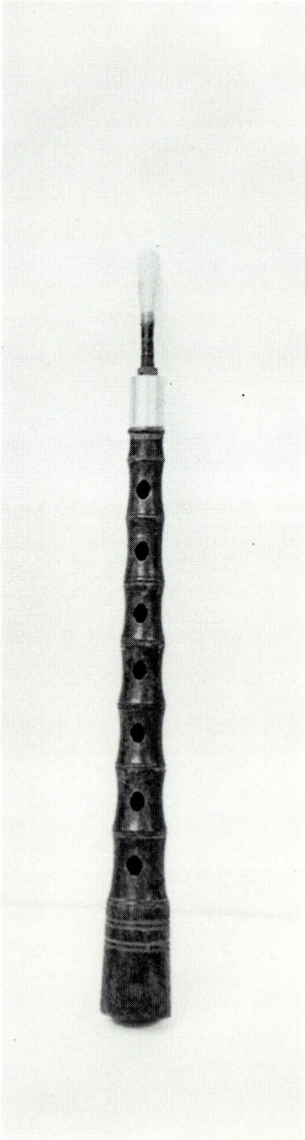

578. Shawm, Spain

Plate XVII

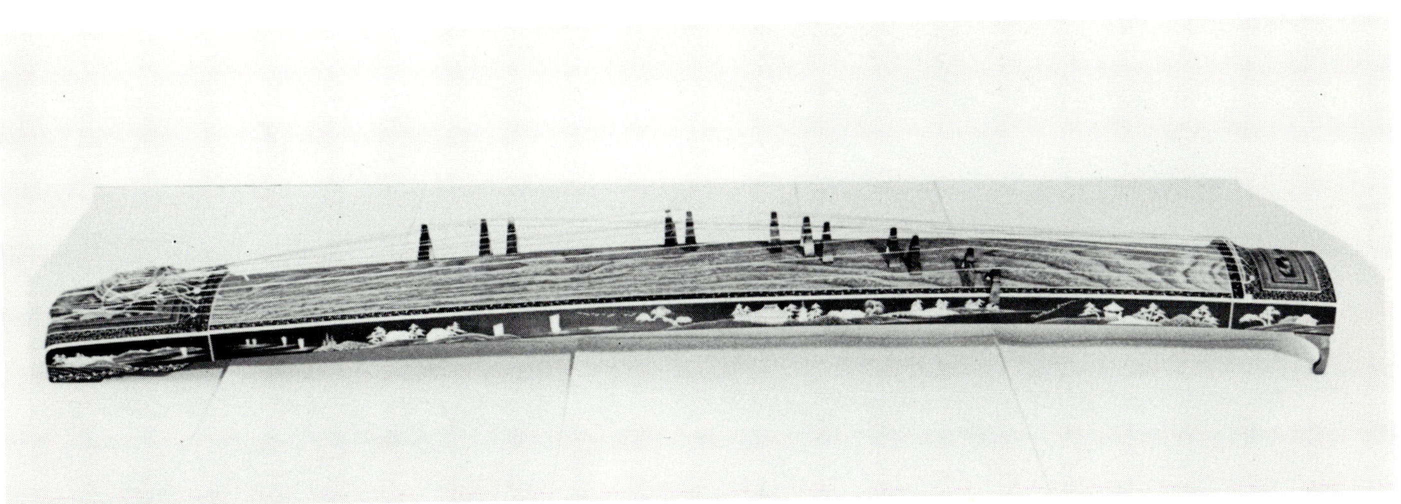

611. Koto, Japan

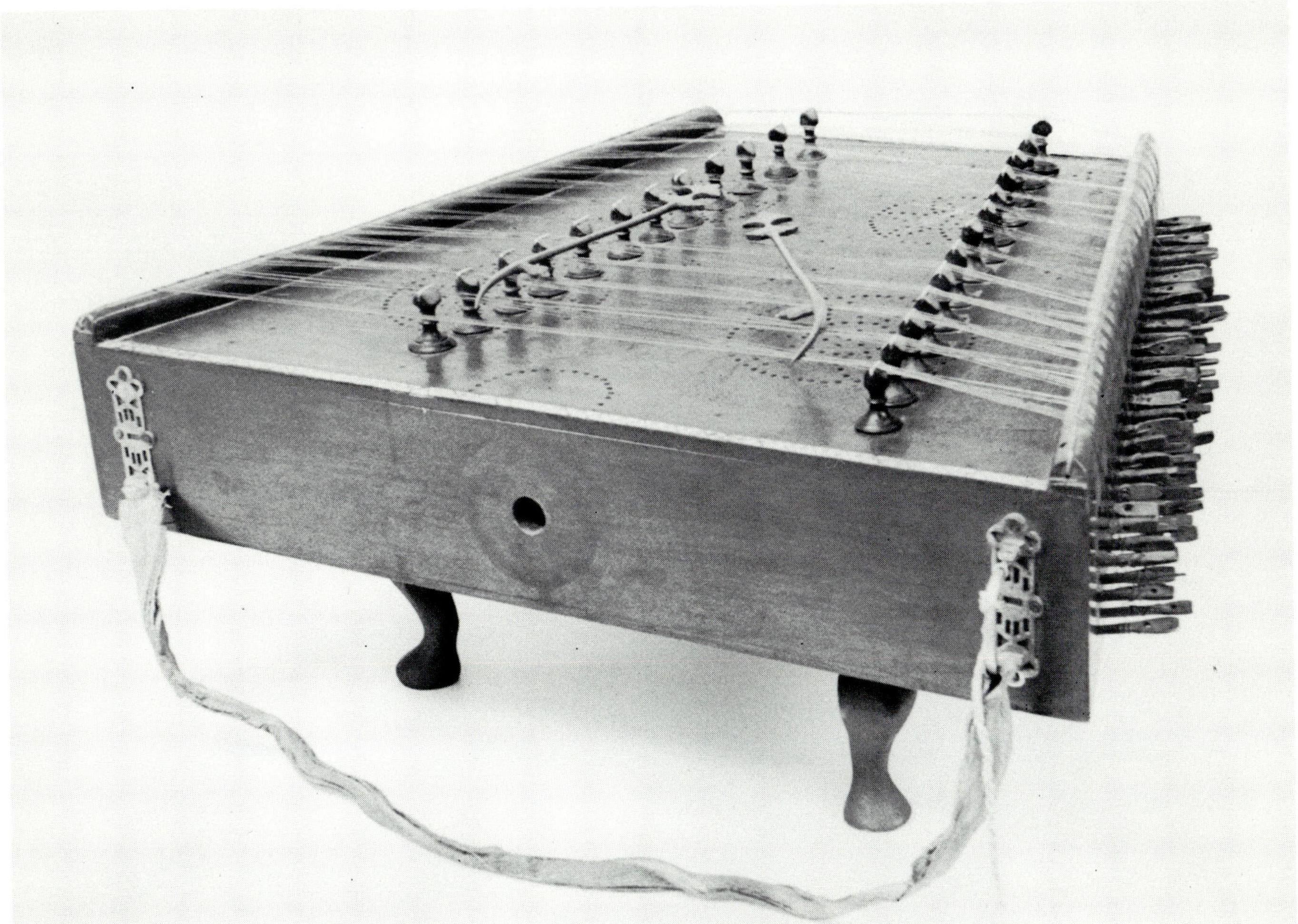

621. Dulcimer, Kashmir

Plate XVIII

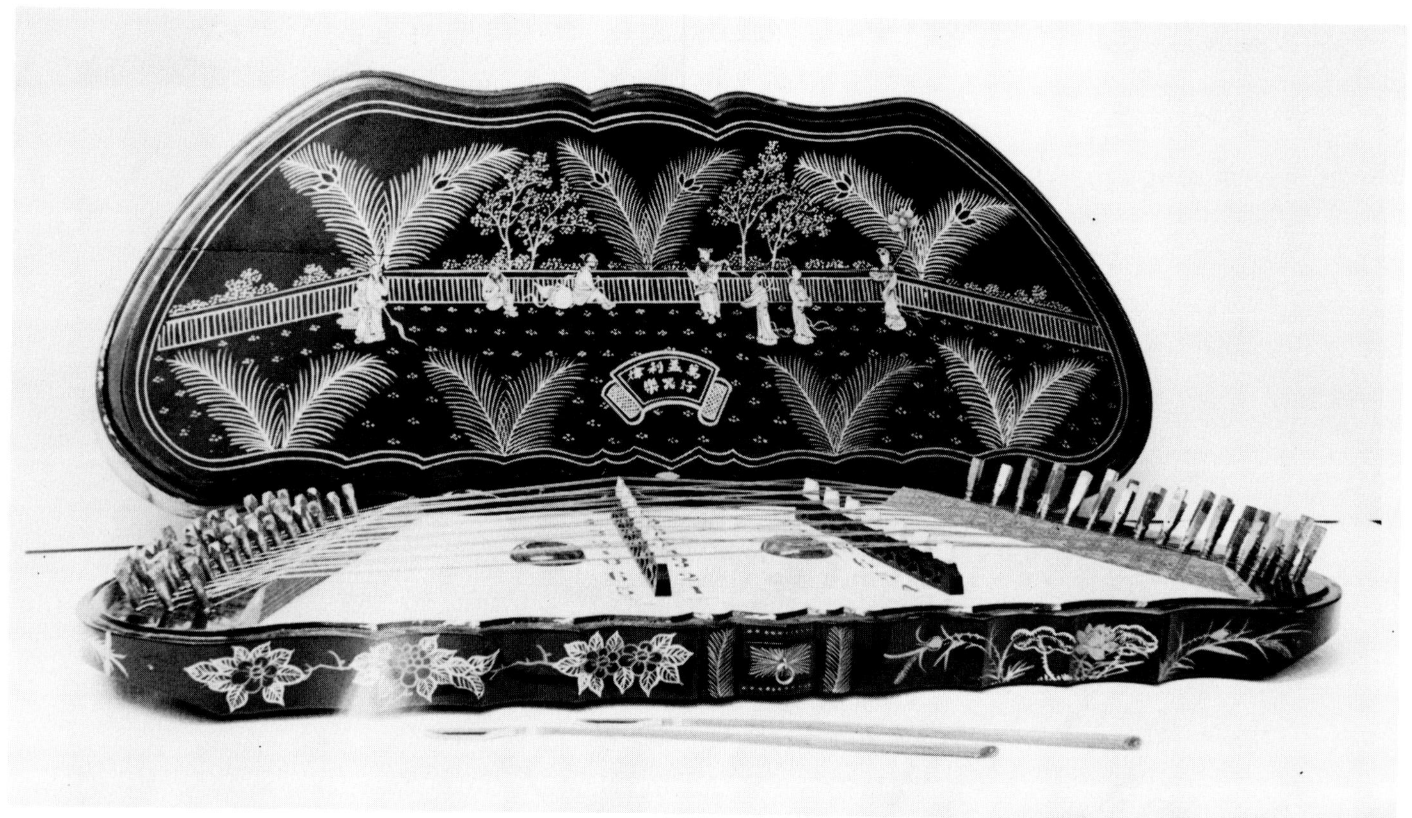

623. Dulcimer, Thailand

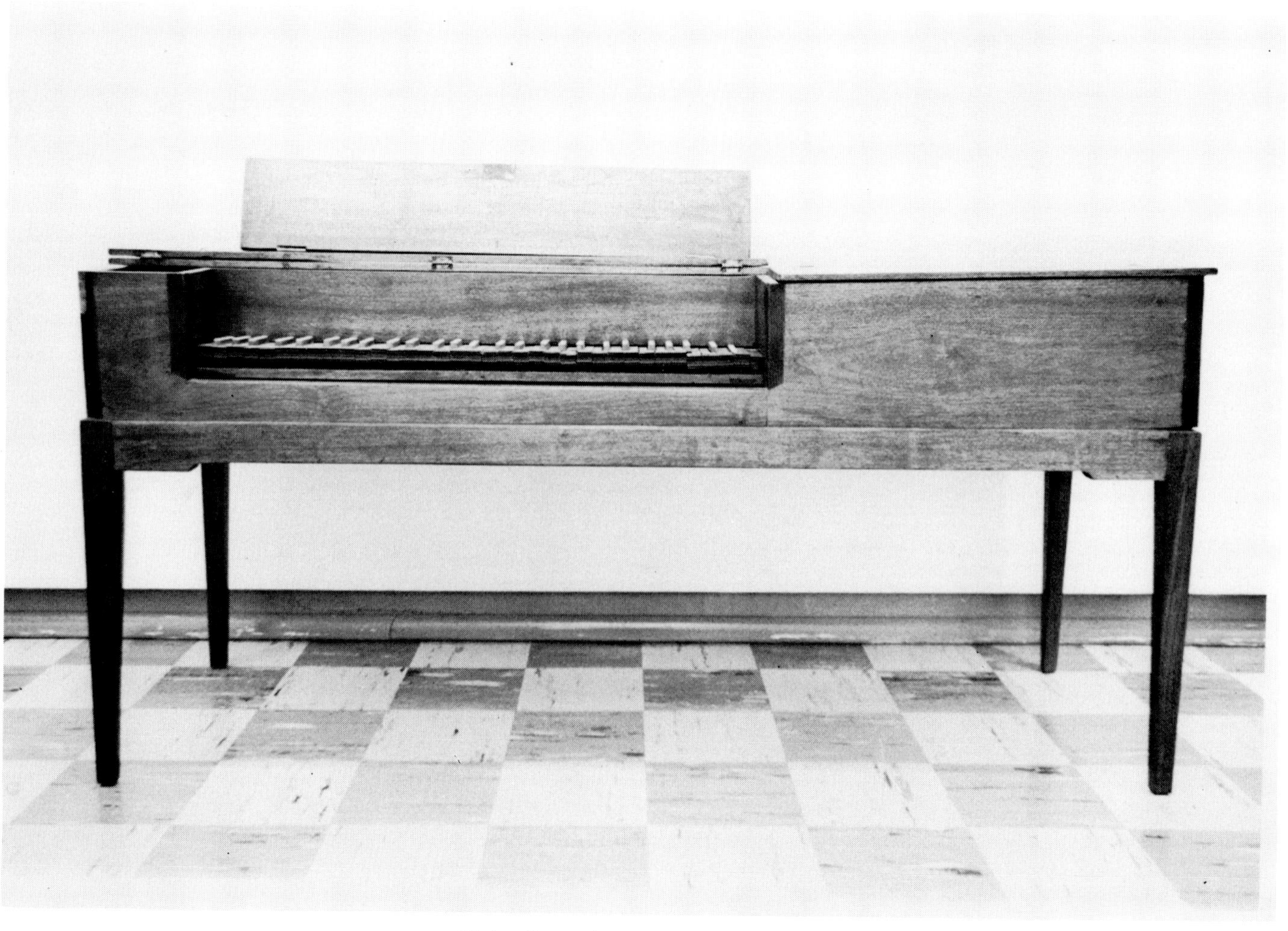

634. Pianoforte, United States

631.   Pianoforte, Austria

641. Moon Lute, Japan

648.   Long Lute, Japan

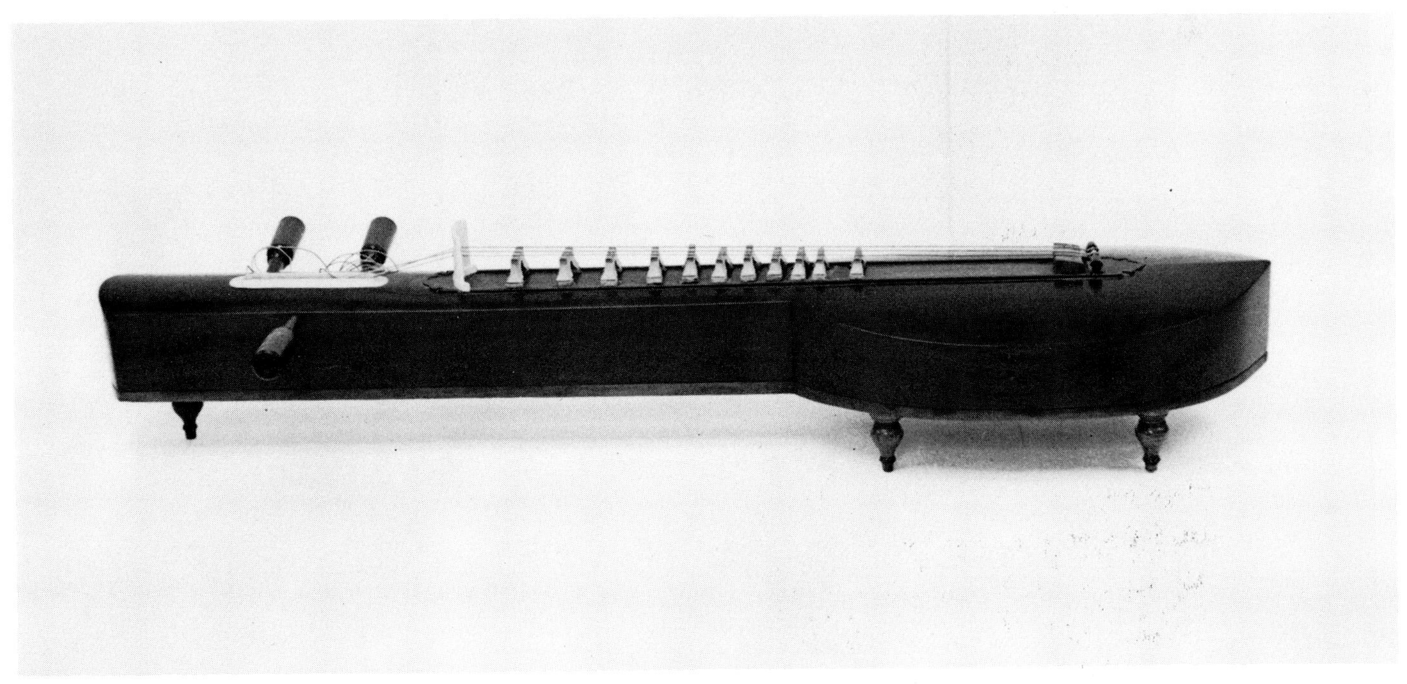

651.   Crocodile Lute, Thailand

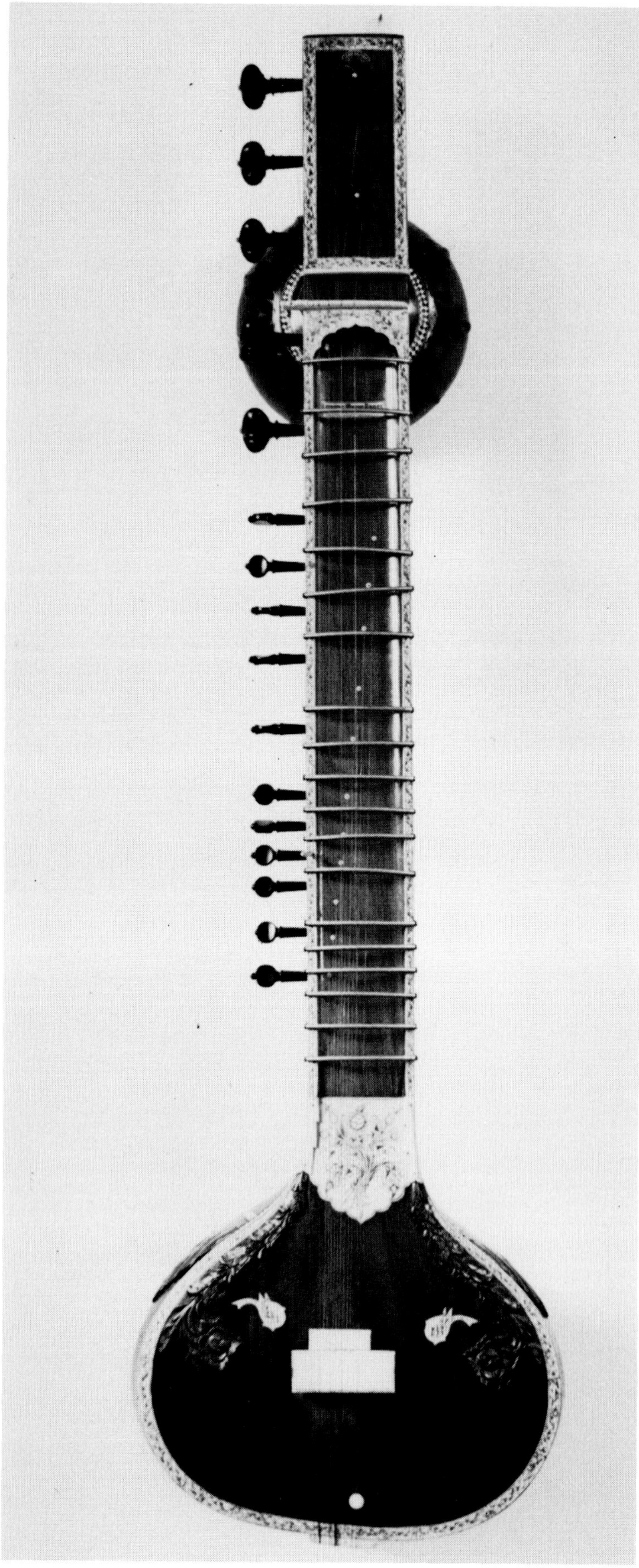

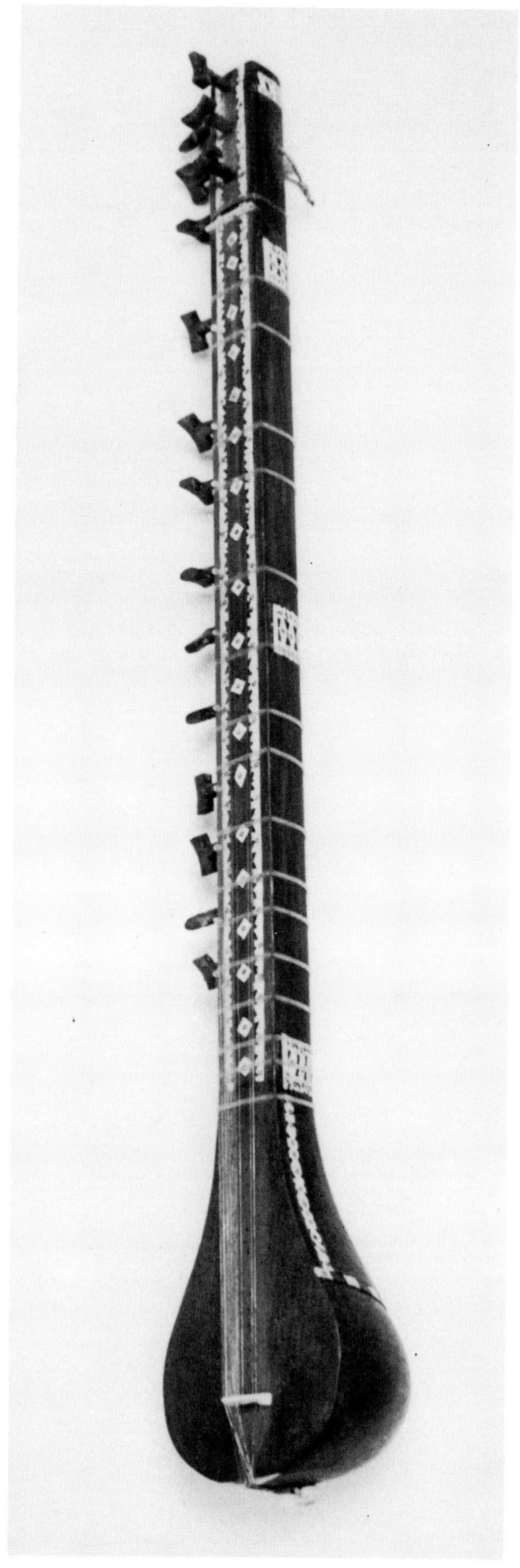

665. Long Lute, India   669. Long Lute, Afghanistan

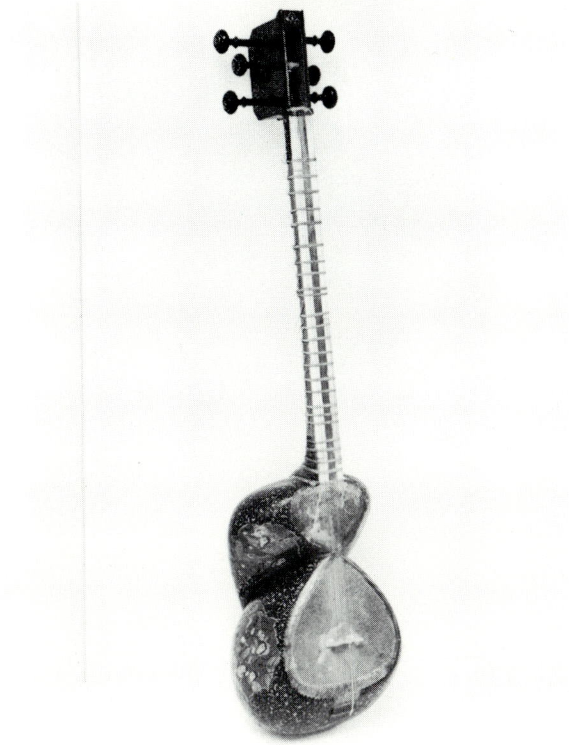

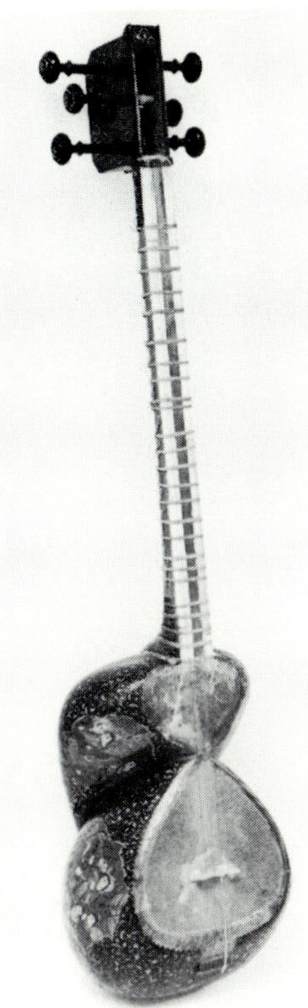

681. Long Lute, Iran

707. Spike Fiddle, Vietnam

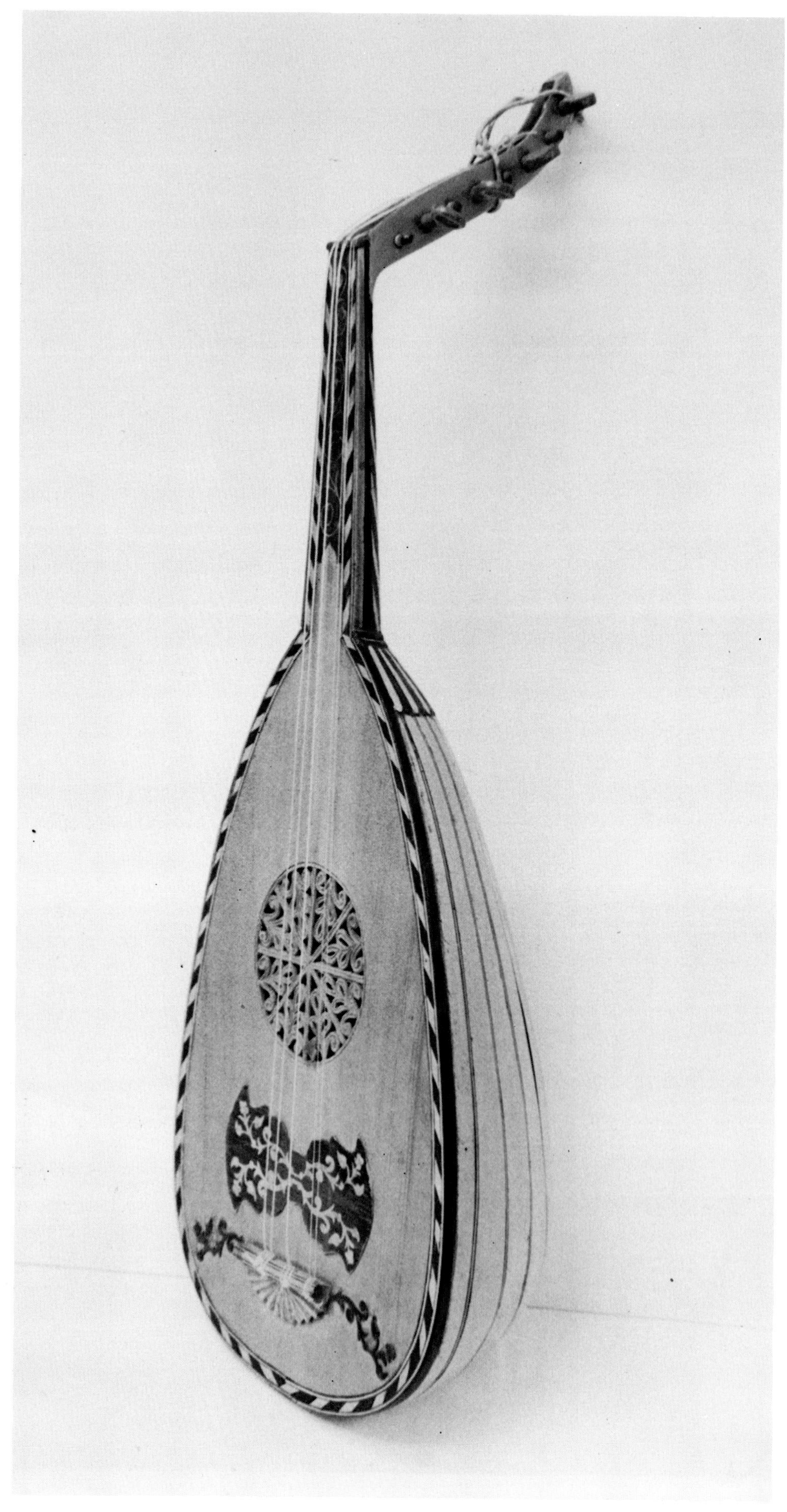

691. Short Lute, Morocco

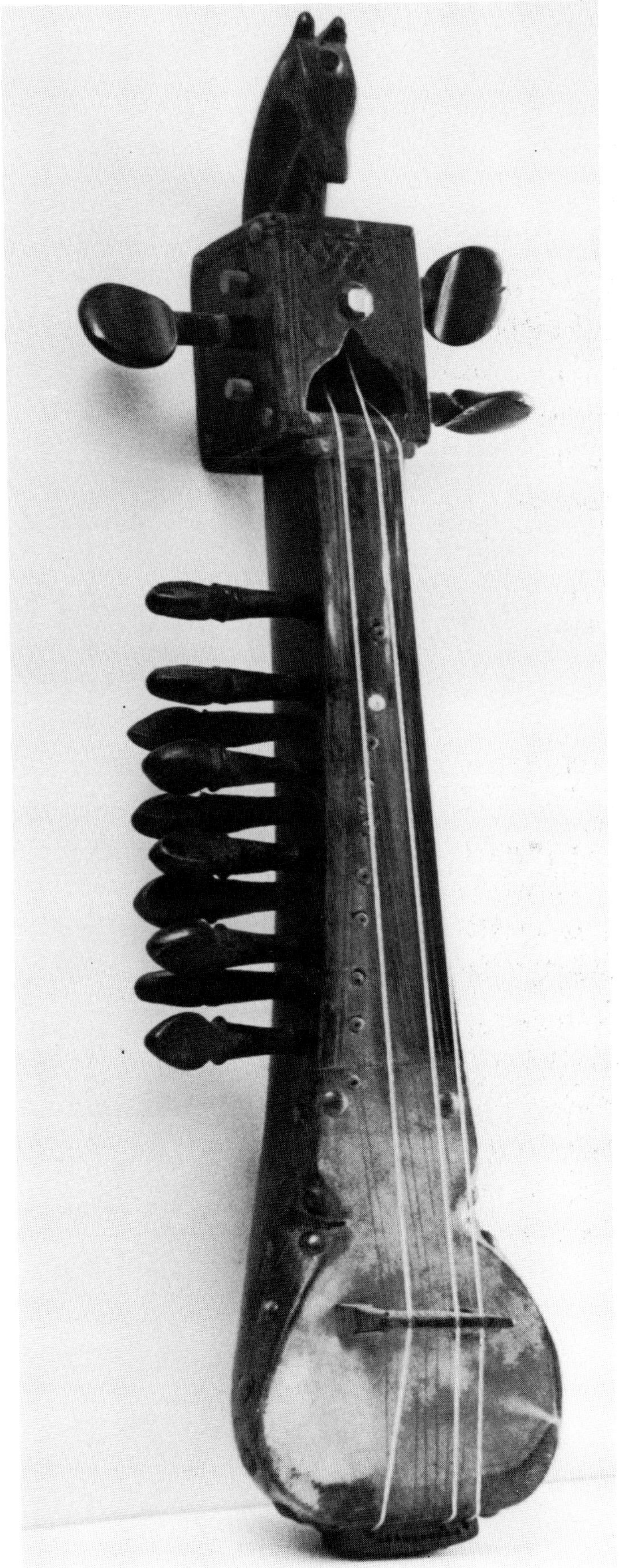

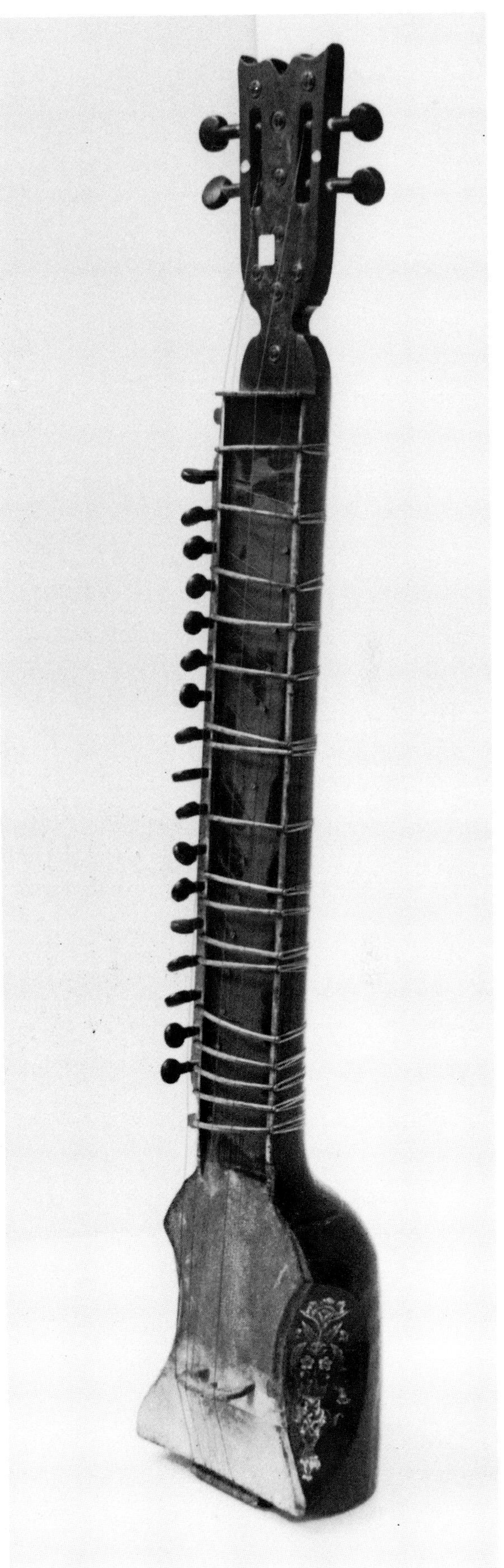

714. Bowed Lute, India   721. Bowed Lute, Kashmir

717. Bowed Lute, India

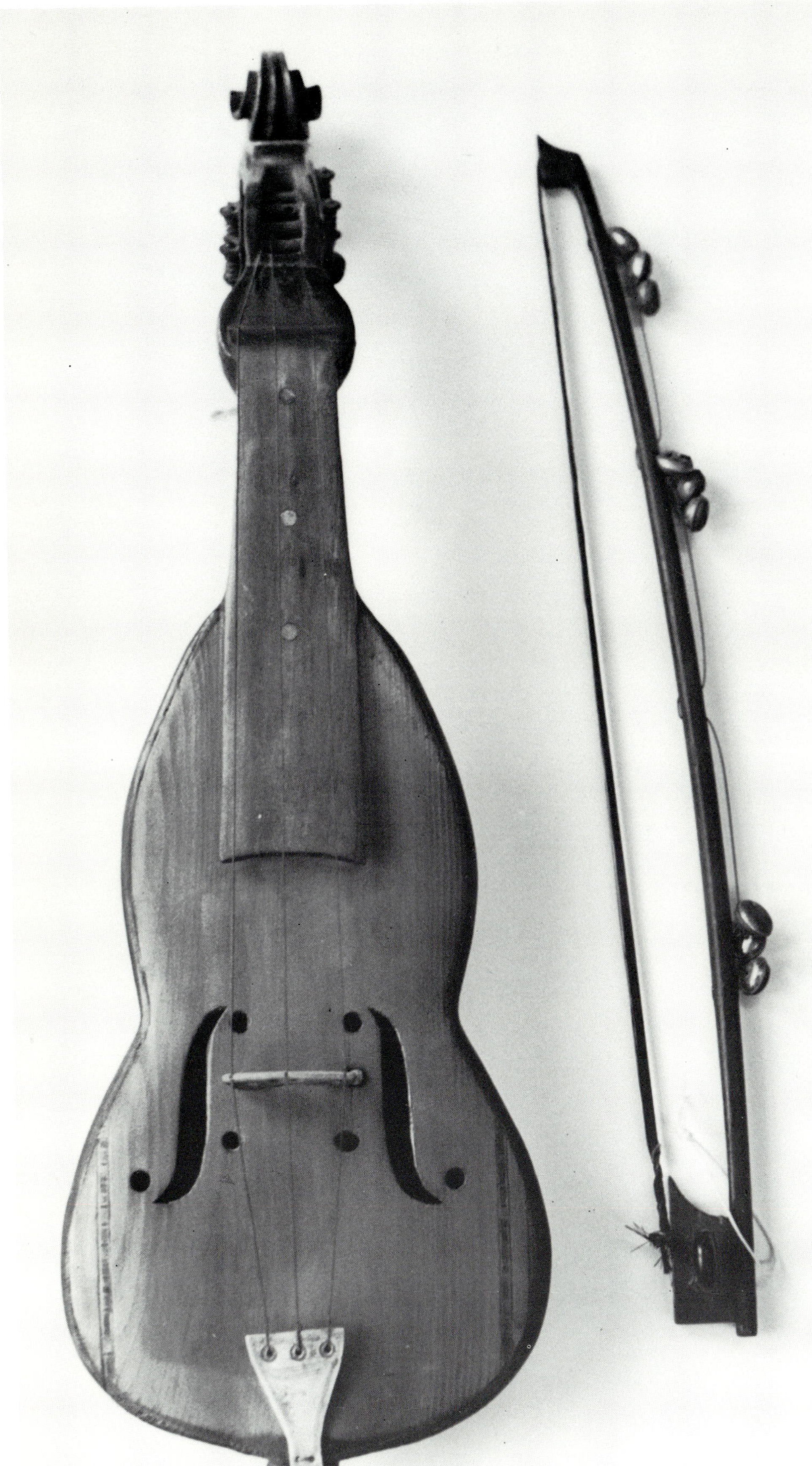

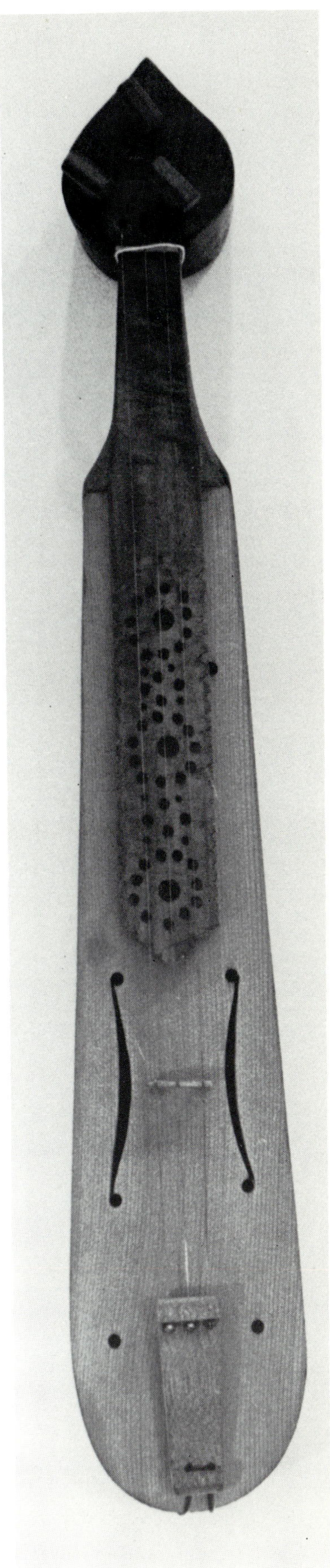

743.   Bowed Lute, Greece

744.   Bowed Lute, Greece

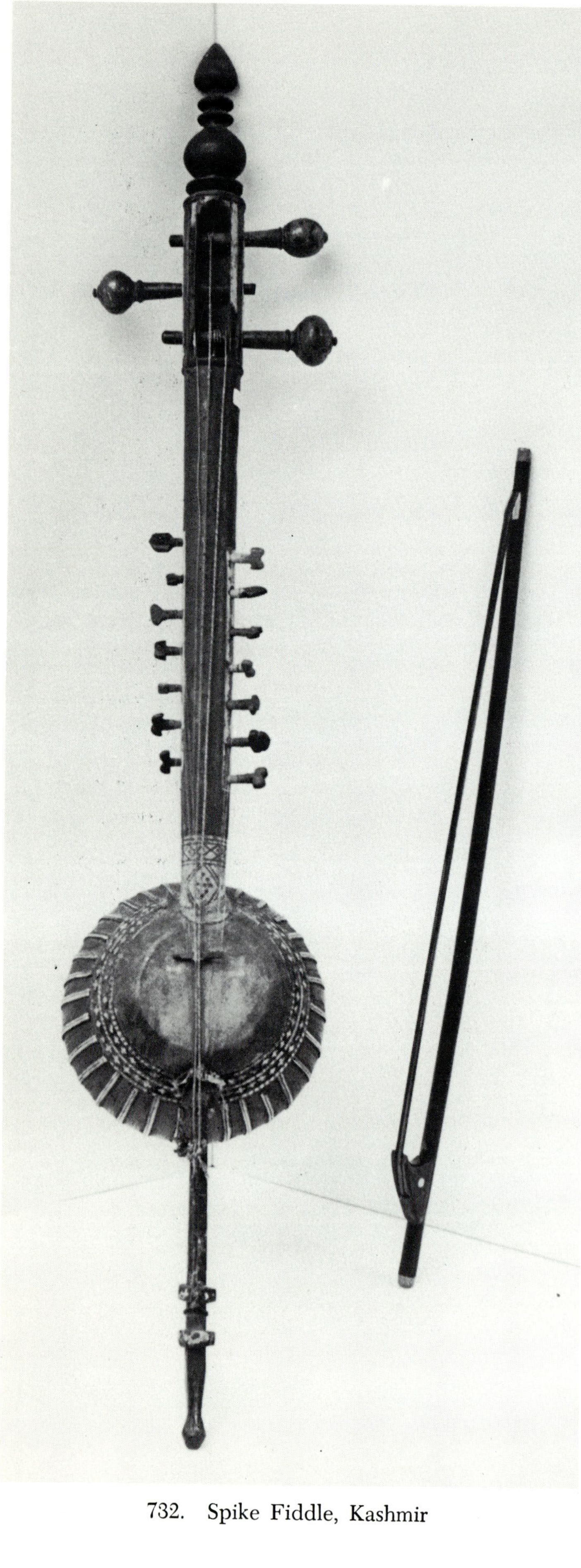

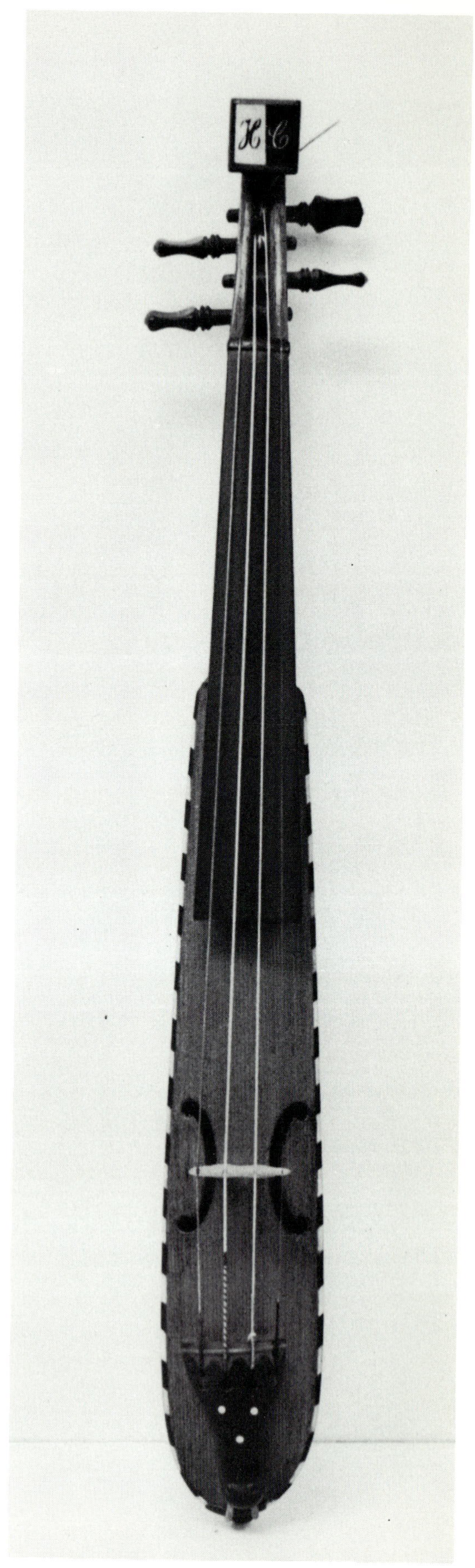

732. Spike Fiddle, Kashmir

750. Bowed Lute, Italy

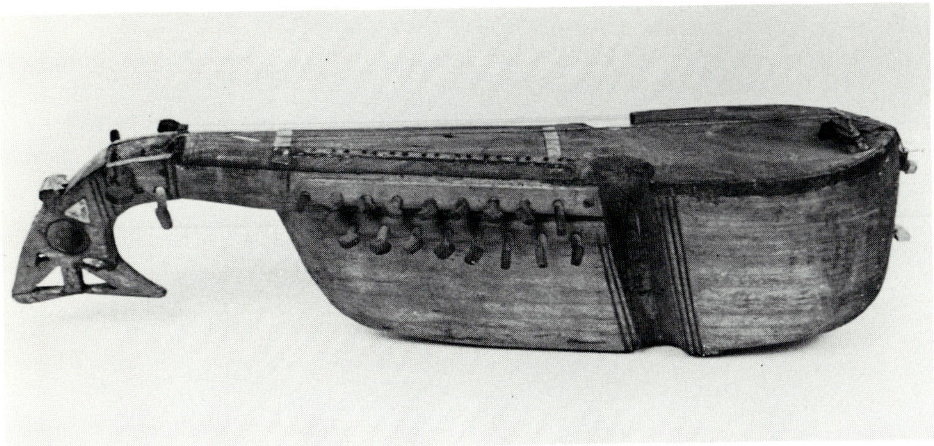

670.   Short Lute, Kashmir

761.   Hurdy-Gurdy, France

761. Detail of Hurdy-Gurdy, France

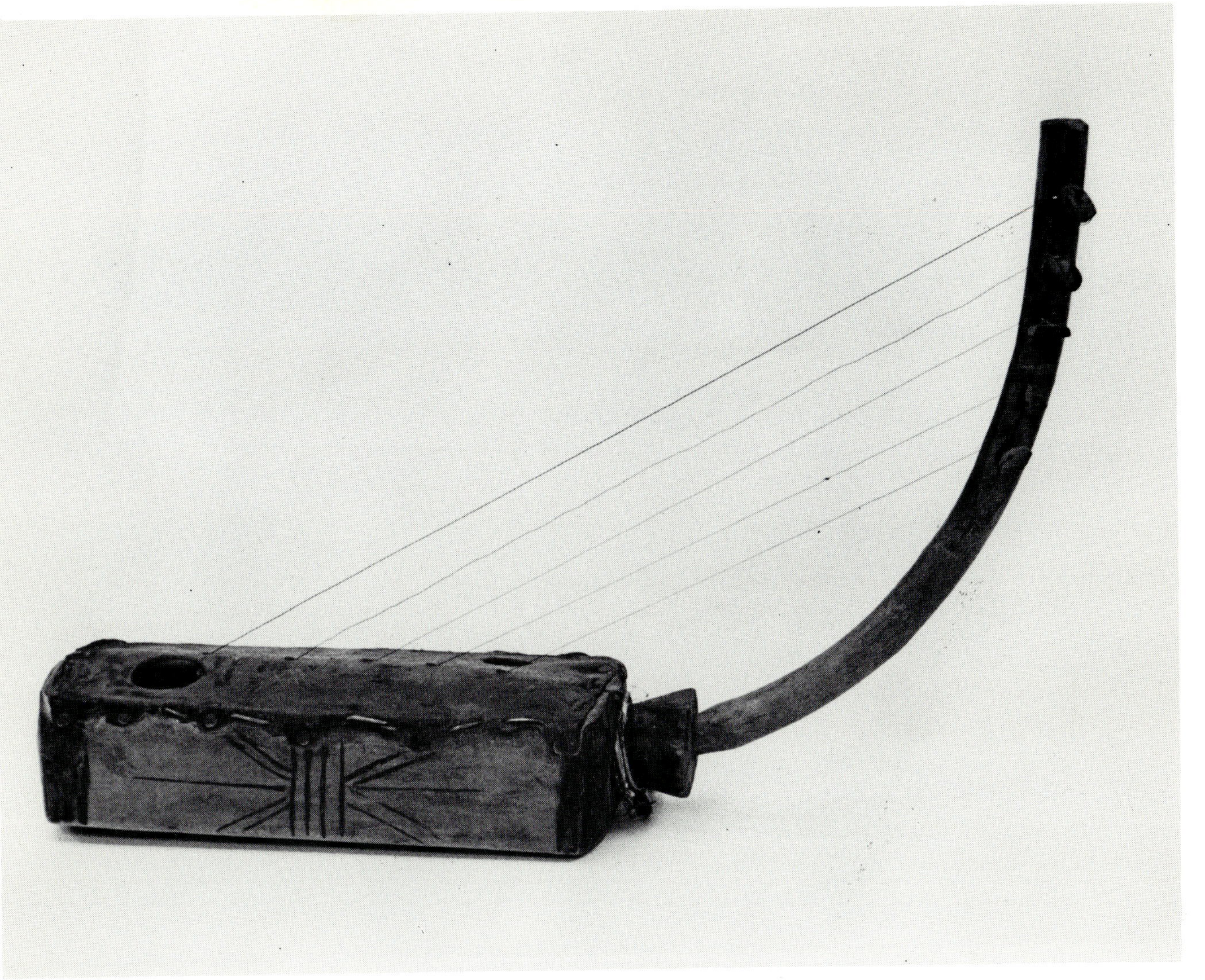

807. Harp, Uganda

803. Harp, Tanzania

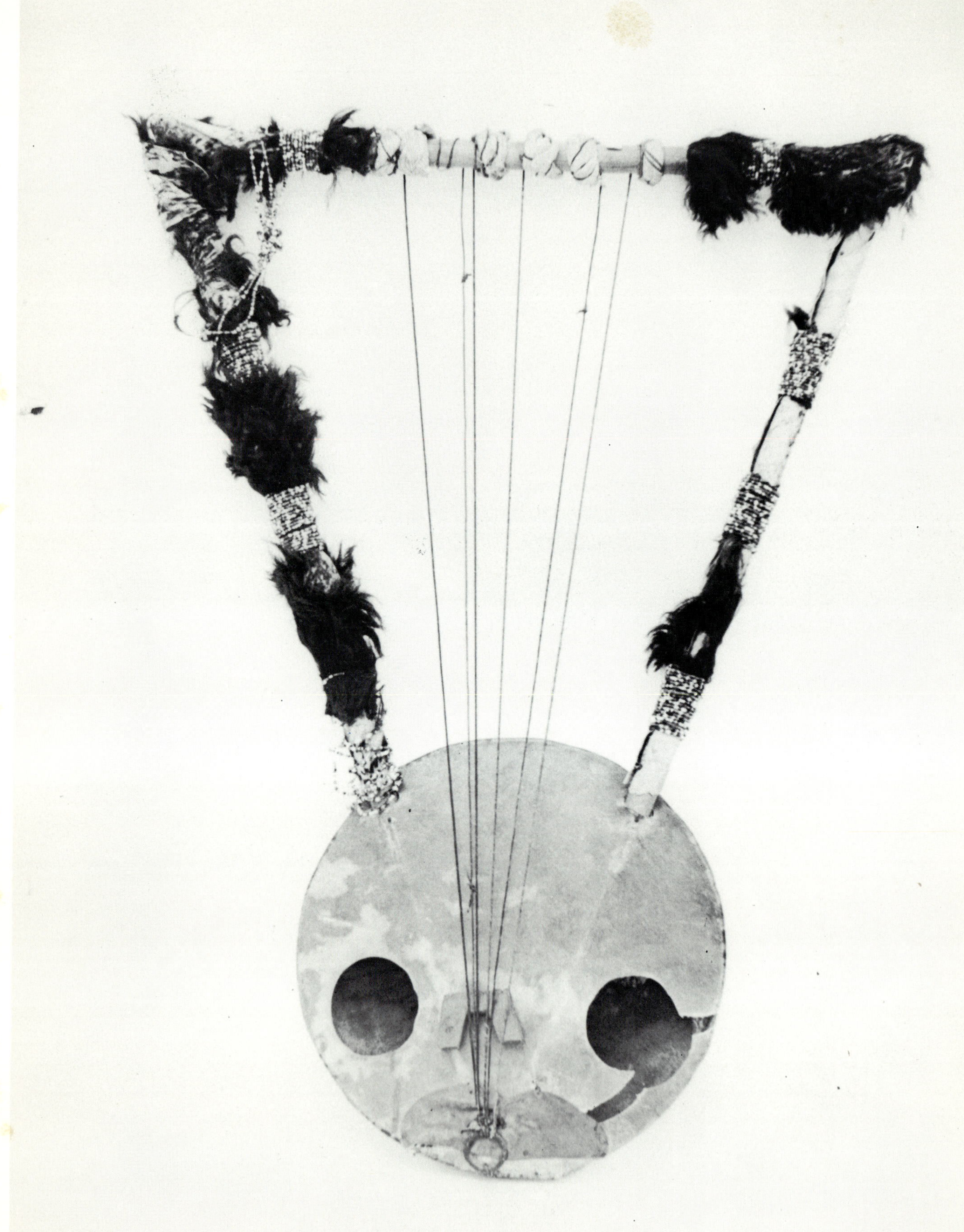

811.   Bowl Lyre, Sudan